I0440952

Build An Email List :
Unlocking Millionaire Wealth Through List Building Mastery

RK. Iskandar

© Riad Karim Iskandar

Table Of Contents

Build An Email List

Chapter 1: Introduction to Email List Building

1.1 The Importance of Building an Email List

In today's digital age, building an email list is an essential strategy for any business or individual seeking long-term success and sustainable growth. An email list consists of a database of individuals who have willingly provided their email addresses, giving you permission to communicate with them directly. This direct line of communication holds immense value and opens up a world of opportunities.

Why is building an email list so crucial? Firstly, it allows you to establish a direct and personal connection with your audience. Unlike social media platforms or search engines, where algorithms control the visibility of your content, an email list puts you in control. You can reach your subscribers' inbox, ensuring your message receives their undivided attention.

Secondly, email marketing boasts one of the highest returns on investment (ROI) among digital marketing channels. With the ability to segment your email list and tailor your messages to specific groups, you can deliver personalized and relevant content, leading to higher engagement, conversions, and ultimately, increased revenue.

Moreover, an email list provides you with a valuable asset that you fully own. While social media platforms and algorithms may change over time, your email list remains a direct channel that you can leverage even if platforms evolve or new ones emerge.

1.2 How Email Lists Can Generate Wealth

Building an email list is not just about amassing a large number of subscribers; it's about nurturing those subscribers and converting them into loyal customers. An engaged and responsive email list can be a powerful driver of wealth generation. Here are a few ways email lists can contribute to your financial success:

a) Repeat Business: By regularly communicating with your email subscribers, you can build trust, establish credibility, and strengthen relationships. This fosters customer loyalty, leading to repeat business and increased customer lifetime value.

b) Product and Service Promotion: When you have a new product or service to offer, your email list becomes a valuable platform for promotion. By crafting compelling email campaigns that highlight the benefits and value of your offerings, you can drive sales and generate revenue.

c) Affiliate Marketing: As your email list grows, you can collaborate with strategic partners and promote their products or services to your subscribers. Through affiliate marketing, you earn a commission for every sale generated through your referral, creating an additional stream of income.

d) Exclusive Offers and Upselling: Your email list provides a unique opportunity to offer exclusive deals, discounts, or special promotions to your subscribers. By leveraging the exclusivity factor, you can drive sales and encourage upselling, maximizing your revenue potential.

e) Joint Ventures and Partnerships: A robust email list opens doors to potential joint ventures and partnerships with other businesses or influencers. By collaborating on mutually beneficial projects, you can expand your reach, tap into new markets, and unlock new revenue streams.

1.3 Overview of List Building Strategies

List building is not a one-size-fits-all approach. It involves employing a combination of strategies and tactics to attract, engage, and convert subscribers. Here's an overview of some effective list building strategies:

a) Lead Magnets: Creating compelling lead magnets such as e-books, cheat sheets, templates, or exclusive content offers incentivizes visitors to join your email list.

b) Opt-In Pages: Designing visually appealing and persuasive opt-in pages that clearly communicate the value proposition and benefits of subscribing.

c) Social Media Integration: Leveraging social media platforms to promote your lead magnets and drive traffic to your opt-in pages.

d) Content Marketing: Producing valuable and informative content through blog posts, videos, podcasts, or webinars to attract and engage your target audience, then inviting them to join your email list.

e) Landing Pages: Creating dedicated landing pages for specific campaigns or promotions, optimizing them for conversions, and including compelling call-to-action buttons or forms to capture email addresses.

f) Exit-Intent Pop-ups: Implementing exit-intent pop-ups on your website to capture the attention of visitors who are about to leave, offering them a last-minute opportunity to subscribe to your email list.

g) Referral Programs: Encouraging your existing subscribers to refer their friends, family, or colleagues to join your email list, rewarding both the referrer and the new subscriber.

h) Quizzes and Assessments: Creating interactive quizzes or assessments that provide personalized results and require email submission for access to the results.

i) Interactive Content: Incorporating interactive elements in your emails or on your website, such as polls, surveys, or interactive calculators, to engage and capture the interest of your audience.

j) User-Generated Content: Encouraging your subscribers to contribute user-generated content, such as testimonials, reviews, or success stories, which not only builds a sense of community but also attracts new subscribers.

k) Collaboration with Strategic Partners: Partnering with complementary businesses or influencers to cross-promote each other's email lists and tap into new audiences.

l) Hosting Virtual Events: Organizing virtual conferences, webinars, or workshops that require email registration, allowing you to capture leads and provide valuable content simultaneously.

m) Leveraging Offline Channels: Collecting email addresses at physical events, trade shows, or through direct mail campaigns to bridge the gap between online and offline marketing efforts.

n) Creating a Sense of Urgency and Scarcity: Utilizing limited-time offers, exclusive discounts, or scarcity tactics to incentivize immediate subscription and capture the fear of missing out.

o) Exit-Intent Surveys: Deploying surveys to visitors who are about to leave your website, gathering feedback and insights while giving them an opportunity to subscribe before exiting.

p) Leveraging Customer Testimonials: Showcasing positive customer testimonials in your opt-in processes or email campaigns to build trust and social proof, encouraging new subscribers to join.

q) Lead Scoring: Implementing lead scoring systems to prioritize and segment your subscribers based on their level of engagement and potential value, allowing you to tailor your communication and offers accordingly.

r) Email Nurture Campaigns: Developing automated email sequences that provide value, educate, and nurture subscribers over time, fostering a strong relationship and increasing conversion rates.

s) Influencer Partnerships: Collaborating with influencers or industry experts to leverage their reach and credibility, attracting their followers to join your email list.

t) Maximizing Email Deliverability and Open Rates: Implementing best practices to optimize your email deliverability and increase the likelihood of your emails being opened and read by subscribers.

u) Analyzing and Optimizing Email Campaigns: Tracking key email marketing metrics, analyzing data, and continuously optimizing your campaigns based on insights and performance results.

v) Retargeting Strategies: Utilizing retargeting techniques to capture the attention of website visitors who did not initially subscribe, giving them a second chance to join your email list.

w) Leveraging Customer Referrals: Encouraging your existing customers to refer others to join your email list, leveraging their positive experiences and satisfaction.

x) Creating Email Courses and Workshops: Designing educational email courses or workshops that provide valuable content and incentivize subscription.

y) Gamifying the Opt-In Process: Adding gamification elements to your opt-in forms or pages to make the subscription process interactive and engaging.

z) Engaging Subscribers with Exclusive Content: Offering exclusive content, insider tips, or sneak peeks to your email subscribers, making them feel special and privileged.

These strategies form the foundation of successful email list building. Throughout this book, we will delve deeper into each strategy, providing step-by-step guidance and actionable tips to help you master the art of list building.

Chapter 2: Setting Clear Goals

2.1 Defining Your Objectives

Before you start building your email list, it is essential to define your objectives. Ask yourself what you want to achieve with your email marketing efforts. This will help you create a clear roadmap for your email list building strategy and ensure that your efforts are aligned with your overall business goals.

Your objectives may vary depending on your business type and industry. Some common goals of email marketing include:

- ✓ Driving sales and revenue
- ✓ Building brand awareness
- ✓ Increasing website traffic
- ✓ Establishing thought leadership and authority
- ✓ Improving customer retention and loyalty
- ✓ Generating leads and conversions
- ✓ Providing value and engagement to subscribers
- ✓ Once you have defined your objectives, make sure they are specific, measurable, achievable, relevant, and time-bound (SMART). This will help you stay focused and track your progress towards achieving your goals.

2.2 Identifying Your Target Audience

To build an effective email list, you must first identify your target audience. Who are the people you want to reach with your email marketing campaigns? What are their demographics, interests, and pain points?

Creating buyer personas can help you understand your audience better and tailor your email marketing efforts to their needs and preferences. Consider conducting market research, customer surveys, or social media listening to gather insights about your target audience.

Once you have a clear understanding of your audience, you can segment your email list to deliver more personalized and relevant content. This can lead to higher engagement and conversion rates, as subscribers are more likely to respond positively to messages that resonate with them.

2.3 Setting Measurable Goals

To ensure that your email list building efforts are effective, it is important to set measurable goals. This will help you track your progress and evaluate the success of your campaigns.

Here are some examples of measurable goals:

- o Increase email subscribers by 20% within the next quarter
- o Achieve a 30% open rate and a 5% click-through rate on email campaigns
- o Generate $10,000 in sales revenue from email marketing efforts in the next month
- o Reduce the unsubscribe rate by 10% within the next six months
- o Increase website traffic from email campaigns by 50% within the next year
- o Setting measurable goals allows you to focus on the key metrics that matter and make data-driven decisions to improve your email marketing strategy. It also helps you stay motivated and accountable, as you have clear targets to work towards.

In conclusion, setting clear goals is a critical step in building a successful email list. By defining your objectives, identifying your target audience, and setting measurable goals, you can create a focused and effective email marketing strategy that delivers results.

Chapter 3: Crafting an Irresistible Lead Magnet

3.1 Understanding the Role of Lead Magnets

In the world of email list building, lead magnets play a crucial role. A lead magnet is a valuable piece of content or resource that you offer to your website visitors or social media followers in exchange for their email addresses. It serves as an incentive, enticing potential subscribers to join your email list.

Lead magnets serve multiple purposes in your list building strategy. They not only capture the attention of your target audience but also showcase your expertise, provide value, and establish trust and credibility. By offering something of value upfront, you demonstrate your commitment to helping your subscribers and create a positive first impression.

3.2 Choosing the Right Lead Magnet Type

To create an irresistible lead magnet, you need to choose the right type of content that aligns with your audience's needs and preferences. Here are some popular lead magnet types:

a) E-books or Guides: Comprehensive written resources that provide in-depth information on a specific topic of interest to your audience.

b) Cheat Sheets or Checklists: Condensed and actionable summaries that help your audience achieve a specific goal or complete a task more efficiently.

c) Templates or Worksheets: Practical tools that simplify a process or help your audience with planning, organization, or tracking.

d) Video Tutorials or Webinars: Engaging and educational video content that demonstrates how to solve a problem or master a skill.

e) Case Studies or Success Stories: Real-life examples and stories that highlight how your product, service, or approach has helped others achieve desirable outcomes.

f) Toolkits or Resource Lists: Curated collections of tools, software, or resources that can benefit your audience in their specific industry or niche.

g) Quizzes or Assessments: Interactive assessments that provide personalized insights or recommendations based on your audience's responses.

h) Exclusive Access or Insider Content: Offering exclusive content, behind-the-scenes access, or early access to new products or features.

When choosing a lead magnet type, consider the preferences and needs of your target audience. Research what types of content they find valuable and what formats resonate with them the most. It's also essential to align your lead magnet with your overall business goals and expertise.

3.3 Creating Compelling Lead Magnet Content

To make your lead magnet irresistible, you must create high-quality and compelling content. Here are some tips for crafting an effective lead magnet:

a) Solve a Specific Problem: Identify a common pain point or challenge that your audience faces and create a lead magnet that provides a solution or addresses that problem directly.

b) Offer Actionable Content: Ensure that your lead magnet provides practical and actionable advice or information that your audience can implement immediately.

c) Showcase Value: Clearly communicate the value your lead magnet provides and how it can benefit your audience. Highlight the key takeaways or outcomes they can expect.

d) Keep it Concise and Digestible: Make sure your lead magnet is easy to consume and doesn't overwhelm your audience. Break down complex information into clear and concise sections.

e) Design Professionally: Invest in professional design and formatting to make your lead magnet visually appealing and easy to read. Use images, charts, or graphics to enhance understanding.

f) Include Your Branding: Incorporate your brand elements such as your logo, colors, and fonts to maintain consistency and reinforce brand recognition.

g) Optimize for Conversion: Place clear and compelling calls-to-action within your lead magnet to encourage subscribers to take the next step and join your email list.

h) Test and Refine: Continuously test and refine your lead magnet based on feedback and performance metrics. Pay attention to the conversion rate and adjust your content or design accordingly.

Remember, the goal of your lead magnet is to capture email addresses and establish a positive first impression with your audience. So, it's essential to create a high-quality and valuable resource that aligns with your overall business goals and expertise.

When creating your lead magnet, consider the following factors:

Your target audience: Think about the interests, needs, and preferences of your audience. What problems do they face, and how can your lead magnet help them overcome these challenges?

Your business goals: Consider how your lead magnet fits into your overall marketing strategy. What specific business goals are you trying to achieve with your lead magnet?

Your expertise: Choose a lead magnet topic that aligns with your expertise and showcases your knowledge and skills. This will help establish trust and credibility with your audience.

Once you've created your lead magnet, it's important to promote it effectively. Here are some ways to do so:

Place it prominently on your website: Feature your lead magnet on your homepage or other high-traffic pages to maximize visibility.

Share it on social media: Promote your lead magnet on your social media platforms, using compelling copy and visuals to attract attention.

Use paid advertising: Consider using paid advertising platforms like Facebook or Google to promote your lead magnet to a wider audience.

Collaborate with other businesses: Partner with other businesses or influencers in your industry to promote your lead magnet to their audiences.

In conclusion, crafting an irresistible lead magnet is a crucial step in building an email list. By understanding your target audience's needs and preferences and creating valuable, high-quality content, you can capture their attention and encourage them to join your email list. Remember to align your lead magnet with your business goals and expertise and promote it effectively to maximize its impact.

Chapter 4: Creating a High-Converting Opt-In Page

4.1 Designing an Eye-Catching Opt-In Page

Your opt-in page is the gateway to growing your email list. It is crucial to design an eye-catching and compelling opt-in page that grabs the attention of your visitors and motivates them to subscribe. Here are some key design elements to consider:

a) Clear and Concise Headline: Your headline should clearly communicate the value of subscribing to your email list. Use persuasive language and make it stand out visually.

b) Engaging Visuals: Incorporate relevant and visually appealing images or graphics that align with your brand and resonate with your target audience.

c) Simple and User-Friendly Layout: Keep your opt-in page clean and uncluttered. Use ample white space and organize your content in a logical and intuitive manner.

d) Color Scheme and Typography: Choose colors that complement your brand and evoke the desired emotions. Select legible fonts that are easy to read across different devices.

e) Mobile-Friendly Design: Optimize your opt-in page for mobile devices, ensuring a seamless experience for visitors accessing your page on smartphones or tablets.

f) Trust Signals: Include trust symbols such as security badges, client logos, or testimonials to instill confidence and credibility.

g) Social Proof: Display social proof elements, such as the number of subscribers or positive testimonials, to demonstrate that others have found value in joining your email list.

h) Progress Indicators: If you have a multi-step opt-in process, use progress indicators to show visitors how far they are in the process and reduce any feelings of friction or uncertainty.

i) Opt-In Form Placement: Position your opt-in form prominently on the page, preferably above the fold, so that visitors can easily locate and engage with it.

j) Exit-Intent Pop-ups: Consider implementing exit-intent pop-ups on your opt-in page to capture the attention of visitors who are about to leave and offer them a compelling reason to subscribe.

Remember, the design of your opt-in page should align with your brand and resonate with your target audience. Test different design elements and layouts to find the optimal combination that maximizes conversions.

4.2 Writing Persuasive Copy for Opt-In Forms

The copy on your opt-in form plays a vital role in convincing visitors to subscribe to your email list. Here are some tips for writing persuasive copy:

a) Clear and Benefit-Oriented Headline: Use a concise and attention-grabbing headline that clearly communicates the value proposition of joining your email list. Focus on the benefits subscribers will receive.

b) Compelling Value Proposition: Highlight the unique benefits, exclusive content, or valuable resources subscribers will gain access to by joining your email list. Emphasize what makes your content different and valuable.

c) Succinct Form Fields: Keep your opt-in form fields simple and minimize the number of required fields to reduce friction. Only ask for essential information like name and email address.

d) Persuasive Call-to-Action: Use action-oriented language for your call-to-action (CTA) button, such as "Get Instant Access" or "Join Now." Make it visually prominent and easily clickable.

e) Privacy Assurance: Address any concerns visitors may have about their privacy by including a short privacy statement near the opt-in form, assuring them that their information is secure and won't be shared.

f) Social Proof and Testimonials: If applicable, include short testimonials or social proof statements near the opt-in form to increase trust and credibility.

g) Urgency and Scarcity: Create a sense of urgency or scarcity by using phrases like "Limited Time Offer" or "Exclusive Content for a Limited Number of Subscribers" to encourage immediate action.

h) Benefit-Focused Bullet Points: Use bullet points to highlight the key benefits of joining your email list. Keep the points concise and specific, focusing on how subscribers will gain value or solve their problems.

i) Compelling Copy Length: Aim for a balance between brevity and providing enough information to entice visitors to subscribe. Test different copy lengths to see what resonates best with your audience.

j) Personalized Language: Use language that speaks directly to your target audience. Address their pain points, aspirations, or specific interests to create a personal connection.

k) Clear Opt-Out Option: While your goal is to encourage subscriptions, it's essential to provide a clear opt-out option and assure visitors that they can unsubscribe at any time. Transparency builds trust.

Remember to review and proofread your copy to ensure it is free of errors and conveys your message clearly. Test different variations of your opt-in form copy to see what drives the highest conversion rates.

4.3 Implementing Effective Call-to-Actions

Your call-to-action (CTA) is the critical element that drives visitors to take the desired action of subscribing to your email list. Here are some tips to make your CTAs more effective:

a) Clear and Action-Oriented Language: Use concise and compelling language that clearly communicates the action visitors need to take. Examples include "Subscribe Now," "Get Started," or "Unlock Exclusive Content."

b) Visual Contrast: Make your CTA button visually distinct from the rest of the page. Use contrasting colors, size, or design elements to draw attention to the button.

c) Placement and Visibility: Position your CTA button prominently on the opt-in page, preferably above the fold. Ensure it is easily visible and doesn't require scrolling to find.

d) Multiple CTAs: Consider using multiple CTAs throughout your opt-in page, strategically placed to capture visitors' attention at different stages of their reading experience.

e) Action-Focused Design: Make your CTA button look clickable by using design elements like shadow, gradient, or a hover effect. This gives visitors a visual cue that encourages interaction.

f) Social Proof: Consider adding social proof near your CTA button, such as the number of subscribers or positive testimonials, to reinforce the credibility and desirability of joining your list.

g) A/B Testing: Experiment with different variations of your CTAs, including button color, text, size, and placement. Use A/B testing to determine which combinations yield the highest conversion rates.

h) Mobile Optimization: Ensure that your CTAs are mobile-friendly and easily clickable on smaller screens. Test the responsiveness and usability of your CTAs across various devices.

Remember, your CTA should be persuasive, visually distinct, and drive visitors to take action. Continuously monitor and analyze the performance of your CTAs to optimize conversions and improve your email list building strategy.

In conclusion, creating a high-converting opt-in page requires careful consideration of design, persuasive copywriting, and effective call-to-actions. By designing an eye-catching page, writing compelling copy, and implementing persuasive CTAs, you can maximize your chances of capturing visitor's attention and driving them to subscribe to your email list.

Chapter 5: Leveraging Social Media for List Building

5.1 Identifying the Right Social Media Platforms

Social media platforms provide immense opportunities for list building and expanding your reach. However, not all platforms are equally effective for every business. It's crucial to identify the right social media platforms where your target audience is most active. Here are some considerations:

a) Research Your Target Audience: Understand the demographics, interests, and online behaviors of your target audience. This will help you determine which social media platforms they are likely to frequent.

b) Analyze Competitors and Industry Leaders: Study your competitors and industry leaders to see which platforms they are using successfully. This can provide insights into where your target audience is likely to be active.

c) Consider Platform Characteristics: Each social media platform has its own unique features and strengths. For example, Facebook offers a wide user base and diverse targeting options, while Instagram is popular for visual content. Choose platforms that align with your content format and marketing objectives.

d) Test and Evaluate: Start with a few selected platforms and test their effectiveness in driving engagement and list growth. Monitor the metrics and user interactions to determine which platforms yield the best results for your specific goals.

5.2 Building a Strong Social Media Presence

Once you've identified the right social media platforms, it's time to build a strong presence to attract and engage your target audience. Here are some strategies to consider:

a) Optimize Your Profiles: Complete your social media profiles with accurate and compelling information about your business, including a link to your opt-in page. Use professional profile pictures and consistent branding elements to create a cohesive image.

b) Share Valuable Content: Create and share high-quality content that resonates with your audience. Offer tips, insights, industry news, and exclusive content that motivates users to engage with your posts and follow your page.

c) Consistency is Key: Establish a consistent posting schedule to maintain regular engagement with your audience. Experiment with different posting frequencies and times to determine the optimal schedule for maximum visibility and user interaction.

d) Engage with Your Audience: Actively respond to comments, messages, and mentions to foster a sense of community and build relationships with your audience.

Encourage conversations, ask questions, and show genuine interest in their feedback.

e) Collaborate with Influencers: Partner with influencers or industry experts who have a significant following and credibility. Their endorsements or collaborations can help increase your reach and credibility, driving more traffic to your opt-in page.

f) Utilize Visual Content: Leverage the power of visual content to capture attention and increase engagement. Use images, videos, infographics, and other visually appealing content formats to convey your message effectively.

g) Utilize Hashtags: Research and use relevant hashtags to increase the discoverability of your content. Hashtags can help your posts reach a wider audience interested in similar topics or trends.

h) Run Contests or Giveaways: Organize social media contests or giveaways that require participants to subscribe to your email list. This not only encourages list growth but also creates excitement and engagement among your audience.

5.3 Encouraging Social Sharing and Engagement

Social sharing and engagement are crucial for expanding the reach of your content and growing your email list. Here are some strategies to encourage social sharing and engagement:

a) Add Social Sharing Buttons: Include social sharing buttons on your blog posts, lead magnet landing pages, and emails to make it easy for your subscribers and visitors to share your content with their networks.

b) Create Shareable Content: Develop content that is highly shareable and appeals to your target audience. This can include thought-provoking articles, informative infographics, entertaining videos, or inspiring quotes.

c) Ask for Engagement: Encourage your audience to like, comment, and share your posts by asking open ended questions or by inviting them to share their opinions, experiences, or tips related to your content. This can spark conversations and increase engagement on your social media posts.

d) Run Social Media Challenges or Campaigns: Create interactive challenges or campaigns that encourage your audience to participate and share their experiences. This not only boosts engagement but also generates user-generated content that can be shared further.

e) Host Live Q&A Sessions or Webinars: Organize live question and answer sessions or webinars on social media platforms to interact directly with your audience. This provides an opportunity to address their questions, offer valuable insights, and encourage them to join your email list for more exclusive content.

f) Engage with Influencers and Relevant Communities: Engage with influencers, industry experts, and relevant communities by commenting on their posts, sharing their content, and participating in discussions. This increases your visibility and encourages them and their followers to check out your content and potentially join your email list.

g) Encourage User-Generated Content: Encourage your audience to create and share their own content related to your brand or niche. This can be in the form of testimonials, reviews, success stories, or creative content. Recognize and share user-generated content, which motivates others to engage and share as well.

h) Run Social Media Ad Campaigns: Utilize social media advertising to promote your opt-in page or lead magnet to a targeted audience. Experiment with different ad formats, targeting options, and ad copies to maximize conversions and list growth.

i) Track and Analyze Metrics: Regularly monitor your social media metrics such as engagement rate, reach, shares, and clicks. Analyze the performance of your social media efforts to identify what strategies are working well and make data-driven adjustments to optimize your list building efforts.

Remember, social media platforms provide valuable opportunities to connect with your audience, expand your reach, and drive traffic to your opt-in page. By building a strong social media presence, encouraging social sharing, and fostering engagement, you can effectively grow your email list and nurture relationships with your subscribers.

.

Chapter 6: Harnessing the Power of Content Marketing

6.1 Developing a Content Marketing Strategy

Content marketing is a powerful strategy for building an email list. By creating valuable and relevant content, you can attract and engage your target audience, establish your expertise, and ultimately drive them to join your email list. Here's how to develop an effective content marketing strategy:

a) Define Your Goals: Determine what you want to achieve with your content marketing efforts. Is it to increase brand awareness, drive website traffic, or generate leads? Having clear goals will guide your content creation and measurement.

b) Understand Your Target Audience: Develop a deep understanding of your target audience's needs, interests, and pain points. This will help you create content that resonates with them and provides value.

c) Choose Content Formats: Select the content formats that align with your goals and resonate with your audience. This could include blog posts, videos, podcasts, infographics, eBooks, or case studies.

d) Create a Content Calendar: Plan and organize your content creation efforts by developing a content calendar. This will ensure a consistent flow of content and help you stay on track with your strategy.

e) Determine Distribution Channels: Identify the channels where you will distribute your content, such as your website, blog, social media platforms, email newsletters, or third-party publications. Tailor your content to each channel to maximize its impact.

f) Set Key Performance Indicators (KPIs): Define the metrics you will use to measure the success of your content marketing efforts. These may include website traffic, engagement rate, social shares, or email sign-ups.

g) Monitor and Adjust: Continuously monitor your content's performance, analyze the data, and make adjustments to your strategy as needed. Experiment with different content types, topics, and distribution channels to find what works best for your audience.

6.2 Creating Valuable and Relevant Content

The success of your content marketing efforts relies on creating content that provides value to your target audience. Here are some tips for creating valuable and relevant content:

a) Conduct Keyword Research: Identify the keywords and topics that are relevant to your audience and align with your business. Use keyword research tools to discover popular search terms and incorporate them into your content.

b) Solve Problems and Answer Questions: Address the pain points and challenges your audience faces by providing solutions and answers through your content. This positions you as a helpful resource and establishes trust.

c) Offer Unique Perspectives: Provide unique insights and perspectives on topics within your niche. Differentiate yourself by offering fresh ideas, alternative viewpoints, or in-depth analysis that sets your content apart from others.

d) Use Storytelling: Incorporate storytelling techniques to make your content more engaging and relatable. Share personal anecdotes, case studies, or success stories that connect with your audience on an emotional level.

e) Keep it Scannable: Format your content for easy readability. Use subheadings, bullet points, and short paragraphs to break up the text and make it scannable. Incorporate visuals, such as images or infographics, to enhance the visual appeal.

f) Incorporate Calls-to-Action (CTAs): Include CTAs within your content to encourage readers to take the next step, such as subscribing to your email list, downloading a lead magnet, or exploring related resources on your website.

g) Update and Repurpose Content: Keep your content fresh by updating it regularly with new information or insights. Repurpose your content into different formats (e.g., turning a blog post into a video or an eBook) to reach a wider audience.

6.3 Optimizing Content for Lead Generation

While creating valuable content is important, it's equally crucial to optimize your content for lead generation. Here are some strategies to optimize your content for capturing email leads:

a) Create Compelling Lead Magnets: Within your content, offer relevant lead magnets that provide additional value to your audience. These can be eBooks, cheat sheets, templates, checklists, or exclusive content that visitors can access by providing their email address.

b) Place Opt-In Forms Strategically: Embed opt-in forms within your content to capture email leads. Consider placing them at the beginning or end of blog posts, within relevant sections, or as pop-ups that appear after readers have engaged with your content.

c) Use Attention-Grabbing Headlines: Craft compelling headlines that grab readers' attention and entice them to continue reading. A strong headline can pique their curiosity and increase the likelihood of them opting in to your email list.

d) Implement Content Upgrades: Offer content upgrades within your blog posts or articles. These are bonus resources directly related to the content readers are consuming. By exchanging their email address for the content upgrade, you can capture valuable leads.

e) Use Exit-Intent Pop-Ups: Employ exit-intent pop-ups that appear when visitors are about to leave your website or a specific piece of content. These pop-ups can offer a last-minute opportunity to entice visitors to join your email list before they navigate away.

f) Incorporate Social Proof: Include social proof elements such as testimonials, reviews, or statistics that demonstrate the value and credibility of your content and encourage visitors to opt in to your email list.

g) Segment Your Opt-In Offers: Tailor your opt-in offers based on the specific content readers are consuming. For example, if someone is reading an article about social media marketing, offer a lead magnet related to social media strategies. This increases the relevance and likelihood of conversion.

h) Test and Optimize: Continuously test different elements of your opt-in forms, such as copy, design, placement, and offers, to optimize their performance. Use A/B testing to compare variations and identify what resonates best with your audience.

i) Offer Content Previews: Provide a sneak peek or preview of the exclusive content subscribers will receive when they join your email list. This builds anticipation and increases the perceived value of subscribing.

j) Highlight Privacy and Benefits: Assure your visitors that their email addresses will be kept secure and emphasize the benefits they will receive by subscribing to your email list. Clearly communicate how being a subscriber will help them solve problems or achieve their goals.

k) Leverage Content Upgrade Pop-Ups: Utilize pop-ups that appear when readers have engaged with your content or have scrolled to a certain percentage of the page. These pop-ups can offer relevant content upgrades as an incentive to subscribe.

By optimizing your content for lead generation, you can effectively capture email leads and grow your email list. Remember to strike a balance between providing valuable content and strategically incorporating opt-in forms and lead magnets to encourage conversions.

Chapter 7: Implementing Effective Landing Pages

Landing pages are standalone web pages designed to persuade visitors to take a specific action, such as filling out a lead capture form or making a purchase. They are an essential component of email list building and can significantly impact the success of your campaigns. In this chapter, we will discuss how to design high-converting landing pages, craft compelling headlines and subheadings, and optimize your landing pages through A/B testing techniques.

7.1 Designing High-Converting Landing Pages

Effective landing pages have a clear and focused purpose, a compelling design, and persuasive copy. Here are some tips to design high-converting landing pages:

a) Keep It Simple: Avoid clutter and distractions by keeping your landing page design simple and clean. Use white space, high-quality images, and a clear visual hierarchy to guide visitors to the desired action.

b) Use Attention-Grabbing Headlines: Craft clear and compelling headlines that convey the value proposition of your offer and entice visitors to continue reading.

c) Highlight the Benefits: Clearly communicate the benefits of your offer and how it will help solve your visitors' problems or fulfill their desires. Use bullet points or a short paragraph to outline the key benefits.

d) Use a Strong Call-to-Action (CTA): Use a clear and prominent CTA that stands out from the rest of the page. Make it easy for visitors to take action by using contrasting colors and placing the CTA above the fold.

e) Use Persuasive Copy: Use persuasive copy that speaks to your target audience's pain points and emotions. Address their concerns and highlight how your offer can help them.

f) Use Social Proof: Include social proof elements such as testimonials, reviews, or trust badges that demonstrate the value and credibility of your offer.

g) Use Visuals: Use high-quality images or videos that support your message and showcase your offer.

7.2 Crafting Compelling Headlines and Subheadings

Headlines and subheadings are critical elements of your landing page copy. They should be clear, concise, and communicate the primary benefit of your offer. Here are some tips for crafting compelling headlines and subheadings:

a) Use Clear and Specific Language: Use clear and specific language that communicates the value proposition of your offer. Avoid using vague or generic language.

b) Use Numbers and Data: Use numbers and data to back up your claims and make them more compelling. For example, "Increase Your Email List by 200% in 30 Days."

c) Use Power Words: Use power words that evoke emotion and encourage action. Examples of power words include "proven," "exclusive," "limited," and "free."

d) Keep It Short and Sweet: Keep your headlines and subheadings short and to the point. Use brevity to capture attention and make your message easy to understand.

7.3 A/B Testing and Optimization Techniques

A/B testing is the process of comparing two versions of a landing page to identify which performs better. Here are some A/B testing and optimization techniques to improve the performance of your landing pages:

a) Test Headlines: Test different headlines to determine which resonates best with your target audience. Use A/B testing to compare variations and identify which generates the most conversions.

b) Test Visuals: Test different visuals, such as images or videos, to determine which supports your message and generates the most conversions.

c) Test CTAs: Test different CTAs to determine which generates the most conversions. Use A/B testing to compare variations in CTA placement, copy, and design.

d) Test Form Length: Test different form lengths to determine which generates the most conversions. Consider reducing the number of form fields to make it easier for visitors to opt-in.

e) Test Page Layout: Experiment with different page layouts to determine which drives higher conversions. Test variations in the placement of elements, such as the headline, form, visuals, and testimonials. Consider different formats, such as long-scrolling pages or multi-step forms, to find what resonates best with your audience.

f) Test Colors and Design Elements: Test different color schemes, button styles, and design elements to determine which combination encourages more conversions. Small changes in design can have a significant impact on user behavior.

g) Test Copy and Messaging: Experiment with different copywriting techniques and messaging strategies to identify what resonates best with your audience. Test variations in the tone, language, and structure of your copy to optimize conversions.

h) Test Mobile Responsiveness: Ensure your landing pages are optimized for mobile devices. Test the responsiveness and usability of your landing pages on various screen sizes to provide a seamless experience for mobile users.

i) Analyze User Behavior: Utilize analytics tools to analyze user behavior on your landing pages. Track metrics such as bounce rate, time spent on page, and scroll depth to gain insights into how visitors engage with your landing pages. Use this data to identify areas for improvement and optimization.

j) Iterate and Improve: Continuously analyze the results of your A/B tests and make data-driven decisions to optimize your landing pages. Implement the insights gained from testing to improve the elements that contribute to higher conversions.

k) Conduct User Feedback Surveys: Gather feedback from users who have interacted with your landing pages. Use surveys or feedback forms to understand their experience, identify any pain points, and gather suggestions for improvement.

By implementing A/B testing and optimization techniques, you can continuously improve the performance of your landing pages and maximize your conversions. Regularly analyze the data, make iterative improvements, and ensure your landing pages align with the preferences and needs of your target audience.

Chapter 8: Utilizing Webinars for List Building

Webinars are powerful tools for building your email list and engaging with your audience in a live and interactive format. In this chapter, we will explore the benefits of webinars, how to plan and promote successful webinars, and strategies for converting webinar attendees into subscribers.

8.1 Understanding the Benefits of Webinars

Webinars offer several benefits for list building and audience engagement:

a) Establishing Authority: Webinars provide an opportunity to showcase your expertise and establish yourself as an authority in your industry. By delivering valuable and insightful content, you can build trust and credibility with your audience.

b) Generating Quality Leads: Webinars attract an audience that is genuinely interested in your topic. The interactive nature of webinars allows you to capture the attention of engaged prospects who are more likely to convert into subscribers.

c) Building Relationships: Webinars provide a platform for direct interaction with your audience. Through live Q&A sessions, polls, and chat features, you can engage with participants, answer their questions, and foster relationships.

d) Showcasing Products or Services: Webinars offer an opportunity to demonstrate the value of your products or services. By showcasing how your offerings can solve your audience's problems, you can generate interest and drive conversions.

e) Repurposing Content: Webinars can be repurposed into other forms of content, such as blog posts, videos, or downloadable resources. This allows you to extend the reach of your content and provide additional value to your audience.

8.2 Planning and Promoting Successful Webinars

To ensure successful webinars that attract and engage your target audience, follow these planning and promotion strategies:

a) Define Your Objective: Clearly define the purpose of your webinar. Is it to educate, generate leads, promote a product, or nurture existing subscribers? Having a clear objective will guide your content and promotional efforts.

b) Choose a Compelling Topic: Select a topic that is relevant to your audience's needs and interests. Conduct market research, analyze customer feedback, or survey your audience to identify their pain points and preferences.

c) Create Engaging Content: Develop a comprehensive webinar outline or script that provides valuable information and actionable insights. Structure your content in a logical and organized manner, using visual aids such as slides or demonstrations to enhance engagement.

d) Select the Right Platform: Choose a reliable webinar platform that offers the features you need, such as screen sharing, chat functionality, Q&A management, and recording capabilities. Ensure the platform can accommodate your expected number of attendees.

e) Set a Date and Time: Consider your audience's time zones and schedules when selecting the date and time for your webinar. Avoid conflicting with holidays or major industry events. Promote the webinar well in advance to maximize attendance.

f) Develop Promotional Materials: Create compelling promotional materials, including email invitations, social media graphics, blog posts, and landing pages. Clearly communicate the value and benefits of attending your webinar to entice registrations.

g) Leverage Email Marketing: Utilize your email list to promote your webinar. Craft engaging and personalized email invitations, send reminder emails closer to the event, and follow up with a post-webinar email that includes relevant resources or offers.

h) Utilize Social Media: Leverage your social media channels to create buzz around your webinar. Schedule promotional posts, use engaging visuals, and encourage your audience to share the event with their networks.

i) Collaborate with Influencers or Partners: Partner with influencers or complementary brands in your industry to co-host or promote your webinar. This can help expand your reach and attract a wider audience.

j) Offer Early Bird Incentives: Encourage early registrations by offering exclusive incentives, such as bonus resources, discounts, or limited-time offers. Create a sense of urgency to drive registrations

k) Provide Clear Registration Instructions: Make the registration process seamless and user-friendly. Ensure that the registration form is easy to fill out and requires only essential information. Clearly communicate the steps to register, including any additional software or tools required for participation.

l) Test Technical Setup: Conduct thorough testing of your webinar platform, audio, video, and internet connection to ensure a smooth and glitch-free experience for both presenters and attendees. Anticipate potential technical issues and have backup plans in place.

m) Practice and Rehearse: Prior to the live webinar, practice your presentation and familiarize yourself with the webinar platform. Rehearse your content, timing, and delivery to ensure a polished and engaging presentation.

8.3 Converting Webinar Attendees into Subscribers

Converting webinar attendees into subscribers requires strategic follow-up and nurturing. Here are some effective strategies to convert webinar attendees into subscribers:

a) Offer Exclusive Content: Provide attendees with additional exclusive content related to the webinar topic. This can be in the form of downloadable resources, bonus materials, or access to a private community or forum.

b) Implement Follow-up Email Sequences: Create a series of automated follow-up emails to nurture webinar attendees. Send a thank-you email immediately after the webinar, followed by a series of emails that provide valuable insights, additional resources, or special offers related to the webinar topic.

c) Share Webinar Replays: Make the webinar replay available to those who registered but couldn't attend the live event. Include a call-to-action in the replay email to encourage them to join your email list for future updates and access to similar content.

d) Personalize Your Communication: Segment your email list based on webinar attendance and tailor your communication accordingly. Send personalized emails that reference their participation in the webinar, address any questions or concerns raised during the event, and offer further assistance or resources.

e) Offer Exclusive Discounts or Promotions: Provide webinar attendees with exclusive discounts or promotions on your products or services. Create a sense of urgency by setting a limited-time offer or a special discount code exclusively for webinar attendees.

f) Engage on Social Media: Continue the conversation and engagement with webinar attendees on social media platforms. Encourage them to share their key takeaways, ask questions, and participate in discussions related to the webinar topic. Direct them to your email list for further updates and valuable content.

g) Request Feedback and Testimonials: Reach out to webinar attendees and ask for feedback on their experience. Use their testimonials or positive feedback to showcase the value of your webinars and encourage others to join your email list.

h) Continuously Provide Value: Once attendees have joined your email list, continue to provide them with valuable content, resources, and exclusive offers. Consistently deliver high-quality content to build trust and keep them engaged with your brand.

By planning and promoting successful webinars and implementing effective conversion strategies, you can build your email list with engaged subscribers who are interested in your offerings and open to further communication.

Chapter 9: Expanding Reach through Guest Blogging

Guest blogging is a highly effective strategy for expanding your reach, establishing authority, and building your email list. By leveraging other platforms and audiences, you can increase your visibility and attract new subscribers. In this chapter, we will explore how to find relevant guest blogging opportunities, pitch compelling guest blog post ideas, and optimize author bios for lead generation.

9.1 Finding Relevant Guest Blogging Opportunities

Finding the right guest blogging opportunities is crucial for maximizing the impact of your efforts. Here are some strategies to find relevant guest blogging opportunities:

a) Identify Target Websites: Research websites and blogs in your niche that accept guest contributions. Look for websites that have an engaged audience and align with your target market.

b) Use Search Engines: Conduct targeted searches on search engines using keywords related to your niche along with phrases like "write for us," "guest post guidelines," or "submit a guest post." This will help you discover websites actively seeking guest contributors.

c) Explore Blogging Communities: Join blogging communities and forums where bloggers share guest posting opportunities. Engage with the community, build relationships, and stay updated on new opportunities.

d) Monitor Social Media: Follow influential bloggers, industry experts, and websites in your niche on social media platforms. They often share guest blogging opportunities or mention when they are open to guest contributions.

e) Utilize Guest Blogging Platforms: Explore guest blogging platforms and networks that connect guest bloggers with website owners seeking content. These platforms streamline the process and provide access to a wide range of opportunities.

f) Analyze Competitor Backlinks: Identify websites where your competitors have published guest posts. Use backlink analysis tools to uncover guest blogging opportunities that are likely to be relevant to your niche.

9.2 Pitching Compelling Guest Blog Post Ideas

Crafting a compelling pitch is essential to secure guest blogging opportunities. Here are some tips for pitching guest blog post ideas effectively:

a) Research the Target Website: Familiarize yourself with the target website's content, tone, and audience. Understand their audience's pain points, interests, and preferences to tailor your pitch accordingly.

b) Develop Unique and Relevant Ideas: Brainstorm unique and valuable blog post ideas that align with the target website's audience and content theme. Focus on providing actionable insights, solving problems, or offering fresh perspectives.

c) Personalize Your Pitch: Address the website owner or editor by name and demonstrate that you have done your research. Show genuine interest in their platform and explain why your guest post would be a valuable addition.

d) Highlight Your Expertise: Emphasize your expertise and credentials related to the proposed topic. Provide examples of your previous work or guest posts to establish your authority and credibility.

e) Outline the Benefits: Clearly communicate the benefits of your proposed guest post, both for the website and its audience. Explain how your post will add value, attract new readers, and generate engagement.

f) Follow Submission Guidelines: Read and follow the website's guest post submission guidelines meticulously. Adhere to word limits, formatting requirements, and any specific instructions provided.

g) Craft a Compelling Subject Line: Grab the attention of the recipient with a concise and engaging subject line.

Make it clear that your email is a guest post pitch and mention the proposed topic or angle.

h) Maintain Professionalism: Use a professional and polite tone throughout your pitch. Be concise, respectful, and express gratitude for the opportunity to contribute.

9.3 Optimizing Author Bios for Lead Generation

Author bios are valuable real estate for generating leads and driving traffic to your email list. Here's how to optimize your author bios for lead generation:

a) Include a Call-to-Action (CTA): End your author bio with a clear and compelling CTA that encourages readers to join your email list or visit a specific landing page. Use action-oriented language and entice readers with a compelling reason to take action.

b) Offer an Incentive: Provide an incentive for readers to subscribe to your email list. This could be a free ebook, a checklist, a webinar, or any other valuable resource that aligns with the topic of your guest blog post.

c) Use a Short and Engaging Bio: Keep your author bio concise, highlighting your expertise and mentioning any relevant accomplishments or credentials. Make it engaging and personable to connect with readers on a personal level.

d) Include Social Proof: If applicable, mention any social proof such as awards, certifications, or media features. This enhances your credibility and encourages readers to trust your expertise.

e) Add Social Media Links: Include links to your social media profiles in your author bio. This allows readers to connect with you on other platforms and increases your chances of building a stronger relationship.

f) Utilize Trackable Links: Use trackable links in your author bio to measure the effectiveness of your guest blogging efforts. This helps you track the number of clicks and conversions generated from each guest post.

g) Update and Revise Regularly: Periodically review and update your author bio to reflect any new achievements, offerings, or changes in your email list incentive. Keeping your bio fresh and relevant maintains its effectiveness in generating leads.

h) Engage with Readers: Monitor the comments and feedback on your guest blog post and respond to reader questions or comments. Engaging with readers demonstrates your expertise and encourages them to further connect with you.

i) Measure and Analyze Results: Use analytics tools to track the performance of your guest blog posts and the effectiveness of your author bio. Measure metrics such as click-through rates, conversion rates, and the number of new subscribers generated.

By finding relevant guest blogging opportunities, pitching compelling ideas, and optimizing your author bios for lead generation, you can expand your reach, attract new subscribers, and establish yourself as an authority in your niche.

Chapter 10: Running Contests and Giveaways

Contests and giveaways are powerful tools for building your email list, increasing engagement, and generating excitement around your brand. In this chapter, we will explore how to create contests and giveaways with impact, promote them to maximize participation, and effectively convert contest participants into subscribers.

10.1 Creating Contests and Giveaways with Impact

When creating contests and giveaways, it's important to design them in a way that captivates your audience and aligns with your goals. Follow these steps to create impactful contests and giveaways:

a) Define Your Objectives: Determine the purpose of your contest or giveaway. Are you aiming to grow your email list, increase brand awareness, drive website traffic, or promote a specific product? Clarify your goals to guide your contest creation process.

b) Choose the Right Prize: Select a prize that is highly desirable to your target audience. It should be relevant to your brand or industry and align with the interests of your ideal subscribers. The prize could be a product or service from your own offerings or a collaboration with a partner brand.

c) Determine the Contest Type: Decide on the type of contest or giveaway that suits your goals and audience. Some popular options include photo or video contests, sweepstakes, caption contests, or voting-based contests. Consider the logistics, budget, and resources required for each type.

d) Establish Clear Rules and Guidelines: Clearly outline the rules, eligibility criteria, and guidelines for participation. Specify the entry methods, entry deadlines, prize details, and any other relevant information. Ensure that the rules are easy to understand and readily accessible to participants.

e) Leverage User-Generated Content: Encourage participants to create user-generated content related to your brand or contest theme. This helps generate buzz and increases the visibility of your contest. Specify the content requirements and any branding guidelines to maintain consistency.

f) Set a Realistic Timeline: Determine the start and end dates of your contest or giveaway. Allow enough time for participants to enter, engage with the contest, and promote it. Consider running the contest for a few weeks to maximize participation.

g) Add a Viral Component: Incorporate a viral element into your contest to increase its reach and exposure. For example, offer bonus entries for participants who refer their friends or share the contest on social media. This incentivizes participants to spread the word and attracts new potential subscribers.

h) Ensure Legal Compliance: Familiarize yourself with the legal requirements for running contests and giveaways in your jurisdiction. Adhere to laws regarding prize eligibility, age restrictions, disclosures, and any necessary permits or licenses.

10.2 Promoting Contests to Maximize Participation

To maximize participation in your contests and giveaways, you need a well-planned promotion strategy. Consider the following tactics to effectively promote your contests:

a) Leverage Email Marketing: Utilize your existing email list to announce and promote the contest. Send dedicated emails highlighting the prizes, rules, and how to participate. Create a sense of exclusivity by offering early access or additional entries to your subscribers.

b) Tap into Social Media: Leverage the power of social media platforms to reach a wider audience. Share captivating graphics, videos, or sneak peeks of the prizes. Encourage followers to enter and share the contest with their network. Use relevant hashtags and tag influencers or partners who can amplify your reach.

c) Collaborate with Influencers: Partner with influencers or micro-influencers in your niche to promote your contest. They can create content, host giveaways on their channels, or share the contest with their audience. Their endorsement adds credibility and can significantly expand your reach.

d) Utilize Paid Advertising: Consider running targeted ads on social media platforms or search engines to reach a larger audience. Set a budget and carefully select your target demographics and interests to ensure that your ads are shown to relevant users. Use compelling ad copy and visuals to capture attention and drive clicks to your contest landing page.

e) Create Engaging Content: Develop engaging content related to your contest or giveaway. This could include blog posts, videos, infographics, or social media posts that highlight the prizes, showcase participant submissions, or share success stories from previous contests. Use storytelling techniques to generate interest and create anticipation.

f) Utilize Influencer Collaborations: Collaborate with influencers or industry experts to promote your contest. They can create sponsored content, host live streams or Q&A sessions, or offer exclusive insights related to the contest theme. Their endorsement and reach can significantly boost participation.

g) Cross-Promote with Partners: Partner with complementary brands or businesses to cross-promote each other's contests. This allows you to tap into their audience and reach new potential subscribers. Consider joint giveaways or collaborations that offer mutual benefits.

h) Leverage PR and Media Outlets: Reach out to relevant media outlets, bloggers, or podcasters to feature your contest. Offer them exclusive interviews, insights, or behind-the-scenes access to generate buzz. Press releases or guest contributions can help attract attention from a wider audience.

i) Encourage Social Sharing: Make it easy for participants to share the contest on social media by providing share buttons and pre-written captions. Offer incentives such as bonus entries or exclusive content for sharing the contest with their network. User-generated content related to the contest can also be shared on your social media channels to encourage engagement.

j) Utilize Your Website and Blog: Create dedicated landing pages or blog posts that provide all the details about your contest or giveaway. Optimize them for search engines and include compelling visuals and calls-to-action to encourage participation. Use pop-ups or banners on your website to grab visitors' attention and direct them to the contest.

10.3 Converting Contest Participants into Subscribers

While the primary goal of running contests and giveaways is to attract new participants, it's equally important to convert them into email subscribers. Here's how you can effectively convert contest participants into subscribers:

a) Include Email Opt-In as a Requirement: Make email subscription a mandatory requirement for participating in the contest. This ensures that participants willingly provide their email addresses, allowing you to add them to your subscriber list.

b) Showcase Email Benefits: Clearly communicate the benefits of subscribing to your email list. Highlight exclusive content, early access to promotions, or special offers that subscribers will receive. Emphasize how being a subscriber adds value and enhances their experience with your brand.

c) Use Segmented Email Follow-Ups: Segment contest participants based on their interests, demographics, or contest preferences. Send targeted follow-up emails that address their specific needs or preferences. Provide relevant content and incentives to further engage them and encourage them to stay subscribed.

d) Offer a Welcome Email Sequence: Upon subscribing, send a series of welcome emails to introduce new subscribers to your brand, products, or services. Use this opportunity to establish a strong connection, provide value, and showcase the benefits of being a subscriber.

e) Provide Exclusive Content: Reward contest participants who become subscribers with exclusive content or offers. This could be a free resource, a discount code, or early access to new products or services. Make them feel special and appreciated for their participation.

f) Nurture Subscribers with Engaging Email Campaigns: Develop a well-planned email marketing campaign to nurture contest participants-turned-subscribers. Provide valuable content, educational resources, and personalized recommendations. Use automation to send targeted emails based on their preferences and actions.

g) Track and Analyze Results: Monitor the performance of your contest and the conversion rate of contest participants into subscribers. Track metrics such as the number of new subscribers, open rates, click-through rates, and conversion rates. Analyze the data to identify areas for improvement and refine your future contest strategies. Pay attention to the engagement and interaction of contest participants who become subscribers, as this indicates the effectiveness of your email marketing efforts.

h) Maintain Regular Communication: Once participants become subscribers, it's essential to maintain regular communication with them. Send them relevant and valuable content on a consistent basis to keep them engaged and interested in your brand. Use a mix of promotional emails, educational content, and personalized recommendations to nurture the relationship.

i) Implement Personalization: Personalize your email communication based on subscriber preferences, behavior, and demographics. Use their first names in emails, tailor content recommendations to their interests, and segment your email list to deliver targeted messages. Personalization helps create a more personalized and engaging experience, increasing the likelihood of subscriber retention.

j) Continuously Optimize Your Strategy: Regularly review and optimize your contest and email marketing strategies. Experiment with different contest types, prizes, promotion channels, and email content to find the most effective approaches for converting contest participants into long-term subscribers. Test different subject lines, email layouts, and call-to-action buttons to optimize your email conversion rates.

By creating impactful contests and giveaways, promoting them effectively, and implementing strategies to convert participants into subscribers, you can grow your email list while building engagement and excitement around your brand.

Chapter 11: Optimizing for Search Engines

In today's digital landscape, search engines play a crucial role in driving organic traffic to your website and helping you build your email list. By understanding and implementing search engine optimization (SEO) strategies, you can improve your visibility in search engine results pages (SERPs) and attract highly targeted traffic. In this chapter, we will explore how to optimize your website and content for search engines to maximize list building opportunities.

11.1 Understanding SEO for List Building

SEO is the practice of optimizing your website and content to improve its visibility and ranking in search engine results. When it comes to list building, SEO plays a vital role in attracting organic traffic and increasing the chances of converting visitors into subscribers. By implementing effective SEO strategies, you can enhance your website's discoverability and reach a wider audience.

Search engines consider various factors when determining the relevance and ranking of a website. These factors include keyword usage, website structure, backlinks, user experience, and content quality. By aligning your website with these factors, you can improve your chances of appearing higher in search results and driving more targeted traffic to your email list.

11.2 Conducting Keyword Research for Optimal Results

Keyword research is a critical component of SEO that helps you identify the search terms and phrases your target audience uses when looking for information related to your niche. By targeting relevant keywords, you can optimize your content to align with user intent and increase your visibility in search results.

To conduct keyword research:

a) Identify Seed Keywords: Start by brainstorming a list of seed keywords that are relevant to your niche and email list. These are the broad terms or topics that define your industry or offerings.

b) Use Keyword Research Tools: Utilize keyword research tools like Google Keyword Planner, SEMrush, or Moz Keyword Explorer to expand your list of keywords. These tools provide insights into search volume, competition, and related keyword suggestions.

c) Analyze Competitor Keywords: Analyze the keywords used by your competitors to gain insights and discover new keyword opportunities. Tools like SEMrush or Ahrefs can help you identify the keywords that are driving traffic to your competitors' websites.

d) Consider Long-Tail Keywords: Long-tail keywords are longer, more specific phrases that have lower search volumes but often indicate higher user intent.

Incorporating long-tail keywords into your content can help you target a more focused audience and increase your chances of attracting qualified leads.

e) Prioritize Relevance and Search Volume: Select keywords that are not only relevant to your email list but also have a decent search volume. Aim for a balance between competitiveness and search volume to maximize your chances of ranking well in search results.

f) Optimize Existing Content: Identify the pages or blog posts on your website that have the potential to rank for specific keywords. Optimize these pages by incorporating relevant keywords into the title tags, headings, meta descriptions, and throughout the content. Ensure that the keyword usage feels natural and does not compromise the readability or quality of your content.

11.3 Implementing On-Page and Off-Page SEO Strategies

To optimize your website for search engines and list building, it's essential to implement both on-page and off-page SEO strategies.

On-Page SEO:

a) Optimize Meta Tags: Craft compelling and keyword-rich title tags and meta descriptions for your web pages. These elements appear in search results and can significantly impact click-through rates.

b) Use SEO-Friendly URLs: Ensure that your URLs are concise, descriptive, and contain relevant keywords. Avoid using generic or automatically generated URLs.

c) Create High-Quality Content: Develop valuable, informative, and engaging content that aligns with your target audience's needs and interests. Incorporate relevant keywords naturally throughout the content and use proper heading tags to structure your content.

d) Improve Page Load Speed: Optimize your website's loading speed to enhance user experience and search engine rankings. Compress images, minify code, and utilize caching techniques to reduce page load time.

e) Optimize Images: Compress and optimize images to reduce file size without compromising quality. Use descriptive file names and add alt tags to help search engines understand the content of the images.

f) Use Internal Linking: Create a network of internal links within your website to connect related content. Internal linking helps search engines understand the structure and hierarchy of your website while providing users with additional relevant resources.

Off-Page SEO:

a) Build High-Quality Backlinks: Acquire backlinks from reputable and authoritative websites within your industry. Guest blogging, influencer collaborations, and content promotion can help you earn valuable backlinks that boost your website's credibility and search engine rankings.

b) Foster Social Media Engagement: Leverage social media platforms to promote your content and engage with your audience. Encourage social sharing and interaction to increase the visibility and reach of your website, ultimately driving more traffic and potential subscribers.

c) Encourage User Reviews: Encourage satisfied customers or subscribers to leave reviews and testimonials on relevant platforms. Positive reviews not only enhance your online reputation but also contribute to higher search engine rankings.

d) Monitor and Analyze Performance: Regularly monitor your website's performance using tools like Google Analytics and Search Console. Track important metrics such as organic traffic, bounce rate, and conversion rate to assess the effectiveness of your SEO efforts. Use the insights gained to refine your strategies and improve your list building results.

By implementing a comprehensive SEO strategy, you can optimize your website and content to attract organic traffic, improve search engine rankings, and increase your email list building opportunities. Remember to stay up to date with the latest SEO trends and algorithm changes to ensure your optimization efforts remain effective.

Chapter 12: Email List
Segmentation and Personalization

In the world of email marketing, one-size-fits-all approaches no longer suffice. To truly unlock the power of your email list and maximize engagement, it's crucial to implement segmentation and personalization strategies. In this chapter, we will explore the importance of segmenting your email list, effective segmentation strategies, and techniques for personalizing your email campaigns.

12.1 Importance of Segmenting Your Email List

Email list segmentation involves dividing your subscriber base into smaller, more targeted groups based on specific criteria such as demographics, preferences, behavior, or purchase history. Here's why segmentation is vital for successful email marketing:

a) Enhanced Relevance: Segmentation allows you to send highly targeted and relevant content to specific segments of your audience. By tailoring your messages to individual needs and interests, you increase the likelihood of engagement and conversion.

b) Improved Engagement: When subscribers receive content that resonates with their specific interests, they are more likely to engage with your emails. This leads to higher open rates, click-through rates, and overall interaction with your brand.

c) Increased Conversion Rates: Targeted and relevant emails have a higher chance of converting subscribers into customers. By delivering personalized offers, recommendations, or content based on segmentation, you can drive conversions and revenue.

d) Reduced Unsubscribes: Irrelevant or generic content can lead to increased unsubscribe rates. By segmenting your list and delivering content that aligns with subscribers' interests, you can reduce the likelihood of them opting out of your emails.

e) Improved Customer Retention: Segmenting your email list allows you to nurture customer relationships more effectively. By understanding their preferences and needs, you can provide ongoing value and keep them engaged, fostering long-term loyalty.

12.2 Strategies for Effective List Segmentation

To implement effective list segmentation, consider the following strategies:

a) Demographic Segmentation: Divide your list based on demographic factors such as age, gender, location, or occupation. This segmentation allows you to tailor your messaging and offers to specific groups.

b) Behavioral Segmentation: Segment subscribers based on their interactions with your emails, website, or previous purchases. This can include segmentation based on browsing behavior, engagement level, purchase history, or specific actions taken.

c) Preference-Based Segmentation: Allow subscribers to indicate their preferences during the sign-up process or through preference centers. Segment your list based on their interests, preferred content types, or communication frequency.

d) Lifecycle Stage Segmentation: Divide your subscribers into different stages of the customer lifecycle, such as new subscribers, active customers, or lapsed customers. This allows you to tailor your messaging to their specific needs and guide them through their journey with your brand.

e) VIP Segmentation: Recognize and segment your most valuable customers or subscribers who have demonstrated loyalty or made significant purchases. Provide them with exclusive offers, early access to promotions, or special perks to show appreciation and foster continued engagement.

12.3 Personalization Techniques for Higher Engagement

Once you have segmented your email list, personalization takes your campaigns to the next level. Here are some techniques to incorporate personalization into your email marketing:

a) Dynamic Content: Use dynamic content blocks to display different content to different segments within the same email. This allows you to customize sections based on subscriber preferences or behavior, ensuring each recipient receives the most relevant information.

b) Personalized Subject Lines: Address subscribers by their first names in subject lines to create a sense of familiarity and increase open rates. Incorporate other personalized elements, such as mentioning past purchases or personalized recommendations, to grab attention and enhance relevance.

c) Tailored Recommendations: Leverage subscriber data to provide personalized product recommendations or content suggestions. Analyze past purchases, browsing behavior, or preferences to offer tailored suggestions that align with their interests and preferences. This not only increases the chances of conversion but also enhances the overall customer experience.

d) Behavioral Triggers: Set up automated email campaigns triggered by specific subscriber actions or behaviors. For example, if a subscriber abandons their shopping cart, you can send them a personalized email reminder with the items they left behind. This targeted approach based on specific behaviors encourages engagement and drives conversions.

e) Personalized Offers and Promotions: Tailor your offers and promotions to individual segments based on their purchase history, preferences, or browsing behavior. By delivering personalized discounts or exclusive deals, you can entice subscribers to take action and make a purchase.

f) Email Copy Customization: Customize the email copy to speak directly to each segment's needs, pain points, or interests. Craft compelling and relevant messaging that resonates with each group, addressing their specific concerns and offering solutions that meet their unique requirements.

g) Testing and Optimization: Continuously test and optimize your personalization efforts to ensure maximum effectiveness. Split test different personalization elements, such as subject lines, email content, or product recommendations, to identify the most impactful strategies. Use data-driven insights to refine your personalization techniques over time.

h) Personalized Surveys and Feedback: Incorporate personalized surveys or feedback requests within your emails to gather valuable insights and understand subscriber preferences better. This information can help you further refine your segmentation and personalization strategies, ensuring you deliver the most relevant content.

Remember, effective personalization goes beyond simply inserting a subscriber's name into an email. It involves understanding their individual needs, preferences, and behaviors to deliver highly targeted and meaningful content that resonates with them.

By implementing segmentation and personalization techniques in your email marketing, you can create more engaging and relevant campaigns that drive higher open rates, click-through rates, conversions, and overall subscriber satisfaction.

Chapter 13: Implementing

Effective Email Automation

In the world of email marketing, automation is a powerful tool that can streamline your list building process, nurture your subscribers, and drive engagement and conversions. In this chapter, we will explore the power of email automation, how to set up automated welcome sequences, and the benefits of implementing drip campaigns.

13.1 Understanding the Power of Email Automation

Email automation allows you to send targeted and personalized emails to your subscribers based on predefined triggers, actions, or specific time intervals. It eliminates the need for manual intervention, saving you time and effort while delivering timely and relevant content to your audience. Here's why email automation is essential:

a) Time Efficiency: With automation, you can set up email sequences in advance, ensuring that your subscribers receive timely messages without requiring manual effort for each send. This frees up your time to focus on other aspects of your business.

b) Personalization at Scale: Automation enables you to deliver personalized content to individual subscribers or segments based on their actions, preferences, or lifecycle stage. This personal touch helps to build stronger connections with your audience and enhances engagement.

c) Increased Engagement and Conversions: By delivering targeted and timely emails, automation helps nurture your subscribers, keeping them engaged with your brand. This can lead to higher open rates, click-through rates, and ultimately, increased conversions.

d) Improved Customer Experience: Automation allows you to send relevant and helpful content to your subscribers at the right time. By providing valuable information, recommendations, or offers, you enhance the overall customer experience and build trust.

e) Scalability and Consistency: As your email list grows, automation ensures that each subscriber receives a consistent onboarding experience, regardless of the size of your list. It enables you to scale your email marketing efforts efficiently.

13.2 Setting Up Automated Welcome Sequences

One of the most critical aspects of email automation is the creation of automated welcome sequences. Welcome sequences are triggered when a new subscriber joins your email list and provide an opportunity to make a strong first impression. Here's how to set up an effective automated welcome sequence:

a) Welcome Email: Send a personalized welcome email immediately after someone joins your list. Express gratitude, introduce your brand, and provide a clear overview of what subscribers can expect from your emails.

b) Introduction and Storytelling: Use subsequent emails in the sequence to share more about your brand's story, values, and mission. Connect with your audience on a deeper level and establish a sense of trust and authenticity.

c) Deliver Value: Provide valuable content or resources that align with subscribers' interests and needs. This could include blog posts, ebooks, guides, or exclusive content that helps them solve a problem or achieve a goal.

d) Call-to-Action: Include relevant call-to-action buttons or links in your welcome sequence to encourage subscribers to take the next step. This could be signing up for a webinar, following you on social media, or making a purchase.

e) Segmentation Opportunities: Integrate segmentation into your welcome sequence by asking subscribers to provide additional information about their preferences or interests. This helps you tailor future emails to their specific needs.

Remember to test and optimize your welcome sequence over time to ensure its effectiveness in engaging and converting new subscribers.

13.3 Nurturing Subscribers with Drip Campaigns

Drip campaigns are a type of automated email series designed to nurture subscribers over time. They are sent at pre-determined intervals and deliver a sequence of relevant and valuable content. Here are some best practices for implementing effective drip campaigns:

a) Define Campaign Goals: Determine the objective of your drip campaign. It could be to educate, onboard, upsell, or re-engage subscribers. Clearly define your goals to ensure your campaign aligns with your desired outcomes.

b) Segment Your Audience: Segment your audience based on relevant criteria such as interests, purchase history, or engagement level. This allows you to deliver targeted content that resonates with each segment.

c) Map Out the Campaign Flow: Create a clear and logical flow for your drip campaign, outlining the sequence of emails and the timing between each email. Consider the frequency of emails and the duration of the campaign to strike the right balance between staying top of mind and avoiding overwhelming subscribers.

d) Provide Value at Each Stage: Each email in your drip campaign should deliver value to your subscribers. This could include educational content, exclusive offers, case studies, customer testimonials, or helpful tips and advice. Keep your content relevant and engaging to maintain subscribers' interest.

e) Incorporate Calls-to-Action: Include relevant calls-to-action (CTAs) in your drip campaign to encourage subscribers to take desired actions. Whether it's directing them to visit your website, make a purchase, sign up for a webinar, or download a resource, strategically place CTAs to guide subscribers toward conversion.

f) Personalize the Content: Leverage the data you have on your subscribers to personalize the content of your drip campaign. Address subscribers by their names, reference their previous purchases or interactions, and tailor the messaging to their specific interests. Personalization enhances engagement and strengthens the connection with your audience.

g) Monitor and Optimize: Regularly monitor the performance of your drip campaign. Track key metrics such as open rates, click-through rates, and conversions to gauge its effectiveness. Use this data to make informed decisions and optimize your campaign over time, adjusting the content, timing, or segmentation as needed.

h) Test and Iterate: Experiment with different elements of your drip campaign, such as subject lines, email copy, CTAs, or the order of emails, to identify what resonates best with your audience. A/B testing allows you to gather data and refine your campaign for maximum impact.

By implementing automated welcome sequences and drip campaigns, you can effectively nurture your subscribers, build relationships, and guide them through their customer journey. Email automation streamlines your communication process, ensuring that each subscriber receives the right message at the right time, leading to increased engagement, conversions, and ultimately, business growth.

Chapter 14: Crafting Compelling Email Copy

In the world of email marketing, crafting compelling email copy is crucial for capturing your subscribers' attention, engaging them, and driving desired actions. In this chapter, we will explore strategies for writing attention-grabbing subject lines, creating engaging email body content, and implementing effective calls-to-action.

14.1 Writing Attention-Grabbing Subject Lines

The subject line is the first thing your subscribers see when they receive your email, and it plays a crucial role in determining whether they open it or not. Here are some tips for writing attention-grabbing subject lines:

a) Personalization: Use personalization techniques such as addressing subscribers by their first name or referencing their previous interactions to create a sense of familiarity and relevance.

b) Curiosity and Intrigue: Spark curiosity and intrigue by posing a question, teasing valuable content, or offering a solution to a problem. Make subscribers curious enough to open your email to find out more.

c) Urgency and Scarcity: Create a sense of urgency or scarcity by highlighting limited-time offers, exclusive deals, or upcoming deadlines. Emphasize the need for immediate action to motivate subscribers to open your email.

d) Clarity and Relevance: Ensure that your subject line clearly conveys the main benefit or value of opening the email. Be concise and avoid misleading or clickbait-style subject lines that may lead to disappointment or decreased trust.

e) A/B Testing: Experiment with different subject lines to see which ones perform best. Conduct A/B tests by sending different subject lines to segments of your audience and analyze the open rates to identify the most effective approach.

14.2 Creating Engaging Email Body Content

Once your subscribers open your email, it's crucial to deliver engaging and valuable content that holds their attention. Here are some strategies for creating engaging email body content:

a) Clear and Concise Messaging: Keep your email content focused and to the point. Use short paragraphs, bullet points, and subheadings to break up the text and improve readability. Make your content scannable, allowing subscribers to quickly grasp the main points.

b) Value-Oriented Content: Provide valuable and relevant content that addresses your subscribers' needs, challenges, or interests. Offer tips, insights, tutorials, or exclusive information that they can benefit from. Make sure your content is actionable and easily applicable.

c) Storytelling: Incorporate storytelling techniques to create an emotional connection with your subscribers. Share personal anecdotes, case studies, or customer success stories that demonstrate the value of your products or services.

d) Visual Elements: Include visual elements such as images, videos, or infographics to enhance the visual appeal of your emails. Visual content can help break the monotony of text and convey information more effectively.

e) Personalization: Leverage your subscriber data to personalize the email content. Use dynamic tags to insert subscribers' names, recommend products based on their preferences or previous purchases, or tailor the content based on their specific interests.

f) Mobile Optimization: Ensure your email content is optimized for mobile devices. Most people check their emails on smartphones, so make sure your emails are mobile-responsive, with easily readable fonts, appropriately sized images, and clear call-to-action buttons.

14.3 Implementing Effective Calls-to-Action

Calls-to-action (CTAs) are critical elements in your email copy that guide subscribers towards taking desired actions. Here's how to implement effective CTAs:

a) Clear and Compelling: Make your CTAs clear, concise, and action-oriented. Use strong verbs that encourage subscribers to take immediate action, such as "Shop Now," "Download Your Guide," or "Get Started Today."

b) Placement and Design: Place your CTAs prominently in your email, ensuring they stand out. Use contrasting colors, bold or larger fonts, and appropriate whitespace to draw attention to your CTAs. Make sure they are easily clickable on both desktop and mobile devices.

c) Benefit-Oriented: Clearly communicate the value or benefit that subscribers will receive by clicking on the CTA. Let them know what they can expect or how their problem will be solved by taking the desired action.

d) Multiple CTAs: Depending on the length and purpose of your email, consider incorporating multiple CTAs throughout the email. This allows subscribers more opportunities to engage and increases the likelihood of conversion.

e) Sense of Urgency: Create a sense of urgency to encourage immediate action. Use phrases like "Limited Time Offer," "Only X Spots Left," or "Ending Soon" to motivate subscribers to click on your CTA before they miss out.

f) Test and Optimize: Continuously test different CTAs to determine which ones resonate best with your audience. Experiment with variations in wording, design, placement, and colors. Analyze click-through rates and conversions to optimize your CTAs over time.

Remember, the key to crafting compelling email copy is to focus on delivering value, engaging your subscribers, and guiding them towards taking action. By writing attention-grabbing subject lines, creating engaging email body content, and implementing effective calls-to-action, you can maximize the impact of your email campaigns and drive desired outcomes.

Chapter 15: Harnessing the Power of Video Marketing

In today's digital landscape, video has become an incredibly powerful tool for engaging audiences and delivering compelling content. In this chapter, we will explore the strategies for incorporating video marketing into your email campaigns to enhance subscriber engagement and build a deeper connection with your audience.

15.1 Incorporating Video Content into Email Marketing

Video content has the ability to capture attention and convey information in a dynamic and engaging way. By incorporating videos into your email marketing campaigns, you can create a more immersive and memorable experience for your subscribers. Here are some ways to incorporate video content into your emails:

a) Embed Videos: Embed videos directly into your emails to provide a seamless viewing experience for your subscribers. Many email service providers support video embedding or provide tools to facilitate video integration.

b) Video Thumbnails: Include captivating video thumbnails with a play button in your emails. When subscribers click on the thumbnail, they can be directed to a landing page or a video hosting platform to watch the full video.

c) GIFs and Cinemagraphs: Utilize animated GIFs or cinemagraphs to add movement and visual interest to your emails. These can be particularly effective for showcasing product demonstrations, event highlights, or teasers for longer videos.

d) Video Previews: Instead of embedding the entire video, include a preview or teaser of the video in your email. This can pique subscribers' curiosity and encourage them to click through to your website or landing page to watch the full video.

15.2 Creating Engaging and Informative Videos

To make the most of video marketing, it's essential to create videos that are engaging, informative, and aligned with your brand and marketing goals. Here are some tips for creating compelling videos:

a) Plan Your Content: Outline the key message and objectives of your video. Consider the needs and preferences of your target audience, and craft content that provides value, solves problems, or entertains.

b) Keep it Concise: Attention spans are short, so aim to create videos that are concise and focused. Get straight to the point and deliver your message effectively within a shorter timeframe.

c) Visual Appeal: Pay attention to the visual elements of your videos. Use high-quality visuals, engaging animations, and relevant graphics to enhance the visual appeal and maintain viewer interest.

d) Clear Audio and Voiceover: Ensure that your videos have clear audio and, if applicable, use professional voiceovers or narration to deliver your message effectively. Poor audio quality can negatively impact the viewer's experience.

e) Brand Consistency: Maintain brand consistency throughout your videos by incorporating your logo, color palette, and visual style. This helps to reinforce brand recognition and build a cohesive brand image.

f) Call-to-Action: Include a clear and compelling call-to-action at the end of your videos. Prompt viewers to take the desired action, whether it's visiting your website, subscribing to your newsletter, or making a purchase.

15.3 Using Video to Build a Connection with Subscribers

Video content can be a powerful tool for building a connection and fostering a sense of authenticity with your subscribers. Here are some strategies to utilize video for building a connection:

a) Personalized Messages: Use videos to send personalized messages to your subscribers. Address them by name and speak directly to them, creating a more personal and intimate connection.

b) Behind-the-Scenes Footage: Offer a glimpse behind the scenes of your business or share exclusive insights and updates through videos. This allows subscribers to feel more connected to your brand and builds trust.

c) Testimonials and Success Stories: Incorporate videos featuring testimonials and success stories from your customers. Seeing and hearing real people share their positive experiences can be highly persuasive and create a sense of trust and credibility.

d) Live Streaming and Q&A Sessions: Host live streaming sessions or Q&A sessions via video to interact directly with your audience. This allows for real-time engagement, fosters a sense of community, and builds trust and loyalty.

e) Educational and How-To Videos: Create educational or how-to videos that provide valuable information or demonstrate the use of your products. This positions you as an authority in your industry and builds trust with your subscribers.

Remember to optimize your videos for different devices and email clients, as not all platforms support video playback within emails. Consider providing alternative ways for subscribers to access your videos, such as linking to a dedicated landing page or hosting platform.

Chapter 16: Partnering with Influencers

Influencer marketing has emerged as a powerful strategy for reaching and engaging target audiences. By partnering with influencers, you can tap into their established following and credibility to enhance your list building efforts. In this chapter, we will explore the strategies for identifying and engaging with influencers, leveraging influencer marketing for list building, and measuring the success of influencer partnerships.

16.1 Identifying and Engaging with Influencers

a) Define Your Target Audience: Before seeking out influencers, clearly define your target audience. Understand their demographics, interests, and preferences. This will help you identify influencers whose audience aligns with your target market.

b) Research Relevant Influencers: Conduct thorough research to identify influencers who have a genuine connection with your niche or industry. Look for influencers with an engaged audience, high-quality content, and a positive reputation.

c) Evaluate Influencer Reach and Engagement: Examine the influencer's reach by assessing their follower count and the level of engagement on their posts. Look for influencers who have a substantial and active following.

d) Assess Brand Alignment: Ensure that the influencer's values, aesthetics, and content align with your brand. It's important to partner with influencers whose personal brand complements your brand image and messaging.

e) Engage Authentically: Approach influencers in a genuine and personalized manner. Show your appreciation for their content, share how their expertise resonates with your brand, and explain the potential mutual benefits of collaboration.

f) Establish Mutually Beneficial Partnerships: Craft partnership proposals that outline the value you can offer the influencer, such as exposure to your email list, product giveaways, or affiliate partnerships. Emphasize the win-win nature of the collaboration.

16.2 Leveraging Influencer Marketing for List Building

a) Sponsored Content and Reviews: Collaborate with influencers to create sponsored content or reviews that highlight your products or services. Request that the influencer includes a call-to-action for their audience to join your email list or opt-in for exclusive content.

b) Giveaways and Contests: Organize giveaways or contests in partnership with influencers. Require participants to subscribe to your email list as an entry requirement, allowing you to capture new leads. The influencer can promote the giveaway to their audience, increasing your reach.

c) Guest Content and Co-Creation: Invite influencers to contribute guest content for your blog or newsletter. This provides value to your subscribers while expanding your reach to the influencer's audience. Collaborate with influencers to co-create valuable content, such as ebooks or webinars, that require opt-in to access.

d) Affiliate Partnerships: Establish affiliate partnerships with influencers, offering them a commission for every new subscriber they refer to your email list. This incentivizes them to actively promote your list and drive sign-ups.

16.3 Measuring the Success of Influencer Partnerships

a) Track Email Sign-ups: Monitor the number of email sign-ups generated through influencer partnerships. Use unique tracking links or dedicated landing pages to attribute the sign-ups to specific influencers.

b) Engagement and Conversion Rates: Analyze the engagement and conversion rates of subscribers acquired through influencer collaborations. Assess metrics such as open rates, click-through rates, and conversion rates to evaluate the quality of the leads generated.

c) Cost-Effectiveness: Evaluate the cost-effectiveness of influencer partnerships by comparing the cost per lead acquired through influencers with other list building strategies. Consider the long-term value of the acquired subscribers in terms of customer lifetime value (CLV).

d) Feedback and Referral Patterns: Seek feedback from new subscribers acquired through influencer partnerships. Monitor their engagement with your emails and their referral patterns. Positive feedback and increased referrals indicate the success of the influencer collaboration.

e) Relationship Building: Assess the strength of the relationship built with influencers. Measure factors such as repeat collaborations, influencer loyalty, and the overall impact of the partnership on brand visibility and reputation.

By identifying and engaging with influencers, leveraging influencer marketing for list building, and measuring the success of influencer partnerships, you can amplify your reach, build credibility, and attract targeted subscribers to your email list.

Chapter 17: Conducting Surveys and Polls

Surveys and polls are valuable tools for gathering insights from your subscribers and understanding their preferences, needs, and behaviors. By conducting surveys, you can collect data that will inform your list building strategies and enable you to deliver more targeted and personalized email campaigns. In this chapter, we will explore the use of surveys and polls to gather subscriber insights, craft effective survey questions, and leverage survey data for list growth.

17.1 Using Surveys to Gather Subscriber Insights

Surveys provide a direct and systematic way to gather feedback and insights from your subscribers. By understanding their preferences, challenges, and expectations, you can tailor your email marketing efforts to better meet their needs. Here are some key ways to use surveys for gathering subscriber insights:

a) Demographic Information: Include questions about demographics such as age, gender, location, and occupation. This information will help you segment your email list and deliver more targeted content.

b) Preferences and Interests: Ask subscribers about their interests, hobbies, and preferences related to your industry or niche. This data will enable you to personalize your email campaigns and deliver content that resonates with their specific interests.

c) Challenges and Pain Points: Inquire about the challenges or pain points your subscribers face. This will help you identify their needs and develop content that provides solutions and valuable insights.

d) Feedback on Past Campaigns: Ask for feedback on your previous email campaigns to gauge subscriber satisfaction and identify areas for improvement. This feedback will help you refine your email marketing strategies and deliver more engaging content.

e) Suggestions and Ideas: Encourage subscribers to provide suggestions, ideas, or topics they would like to see covered in your future emails. This input can inspire fresh content ideas and ensure that you are addressing their specific interests.

17.2 Crafting Effective Survey Questions

Crafting effective survey questions is crucial for obtaining accurate and actionable data. Here are some guidelines for creating survey questions that yield valuable insights:

a) Keep Questions Clear and Concise: Use simple and straightforward language to ensure that respondents understand the questions. Avoid ambiguity or complex phrasing that might confuse or mislead them.

b) Use a Mix of Question Types: Include a variety of question types such as multiple-choice, rating scales, and open-ended questions. This allows you to gather quantitative data for easy analysis as well as qualitative data that provides deeper insights.

c) Avoid Leading Questions: Avoid biasing the responses by crafting neutral questions. Leading questions can influence respondents to provide certain answers and compromise the accuracy of the data.

d) Limit the Number of Questions: Keep the survey concise and focused to maximize completion rates. Long surveys can lead to respondent fatigue and decrease the quality of their responses.

e) Test and Refine: Before launching the survey to your entire list, test it with a smaller sample group to identify any issues with clarity, relevance, or technical aspects. Make necessary refinements based on the feedback received.

17.3 Leveraging Survey Data for List Growth

The data collected from surveys can be instrumental in optimizing your list building strategies. Here's how you can leverage survey data for list growth:

a) Segmentation: Analyze the survey responses to identify common characteristics or preferences among your subscribers. Use this information to segment your email list and create more targeted campaigns that resonate with specific segments.

b) Personalization: Tailor your email content based on the survey data. Personalize subject lines, email copy, and offers to align with subscribers' preferences, interests, and challenges.

c) Content Creation: Utilize the survey responses to generate ideas for new content. Address the pain points and topics of interest expressed by your subscribers, ensuring that your email content is valuable and relevant to their needs.

d) Opt-In Incentives: Offer exclusive opt-in incentives based on the survey data. Provide relevant resources, discounts, or content upgrades that align with subscribers' preferences, enticing them to join your email list.

e) Targeted Campaigns: Develop targeted email campaigns that address specific subscriber segments identified through survey data. Create content and offers tailored to their unique preferences and challenges.

f) Feedback Loop: Continuously gather feedback through periodic surveys to track changes in subscriber preferences and adapt your list building strategies accordingly. This iterative feedback loop ensures that your email marketing efforts remain aligned with your audience's evolving needs.

By effectively utilizing surveys and polls to gather subscriber insights, crafting effective survey questions, and leveraging the survey data for list growth, you can enhance your understanding of your subscribers, deliver more personalized content, and attract a larger and more engaged email list.

Chapter 18: Implementing Exit Intent Pop-ups

Exit intent pop-ups are a powerful tool for capturing the attention of visitors who are about to leave your website. By strategically displaying targeted pop-ups when users show exit intent, you can convert potential bounce traffic into valuable email subscribers. In this chapter, we will explore the implementation of exit intent pop-ups, designing effective pop-ups, and offering irresistible opt-in incentives to maximize their effectiveness.

18.1 Capturing Visitors with Exit Intent Technology

Exit intent technology tracks user behavior on your website and detects when visitors are about to leave. This presents an opportune moment to display an exit intent pop-up and entice users to stay engaged. Here's how you can capture visitors with exit intent technology:

a) Choose an Exit Intent Tool: Select a reliable exit intent tool or plugin that integrates seamlessly with your website. There are various options available, ranging from simple plugins to more advanced platforms that offer customization and analytics features.

b) Set Triggers and Behavior Conditions: Configure the exit intent tool to activate the pop-up when certain exit behaviors are detected, such as cursor movement towards the browser's close button or rapid scrolling to the top of the page. Customize the triggers and behavior conditions based on your audience and website analytics.

c) Timing and Frequency: Set the timing and frequency of the pop-up display carefully. Avoid overwhelming visitors with excessive pop-ups, but ensure that the pop-up appears with enough time for them to engage before leaving the website.

18.2 Designing Effective Exit Intent Pop-ups

Designing effective exit intent pop-ups requires careful consideration of visual appeal, messaging, and relevance. Follow these best practices to create compelling exit intent pop-ups:

a) Clear and Eye-Catching Design: Use visually appealing designs that capture attention without overwhelming the user. Use contrasting colors, compelling visuals, and attention-grabbing headlines to make the pop-up stand out.

b) Concise and Persuasive Copy: Craft concise and persuasive copy that clearly communicates the value of subscribing to your email list. Highlight the benefits, exclusive content, or offers that subscribers will receive.

c) Minimal Form Fields: Keep the opt-in form fields minimal to reduce friction and increase the likelihood of conversions. Ask for essential information like name and email address, and consider using single-field opt-in forms for a streamlined user experience.

d) Mobile-Friendly Design: Ensure that your exit intent pop-ups are optimized for mobile devices. Responsive design and mobile-friendly form fields are crucial to provide a seamless experience across all devices.

e) Exit Option: Include a clear and easily accessible exit option within the pop-up. Respect the user's decision if they choose to exit, as forcing the pop-up may negatively impact the user experience.

18.3 Offering Irresistible Opt-In Incentives

To entice visitors to subscribe to your email list through exit intent pop-ups, offer irresistible opt-in incentives that provide value and compel them to take action. Consider these strategies:

a) Exclusive Content: Offer access to exclusive content such as ebooks, guides, or industry reports that are not available elsewhere. Highlight the value and relevance of the content to incentivize sign-ups.

b) Discounts and Promotions: Provide exclusive discounts, promotions, or early access to new products or services. Highlight the savings or benefits subscribers will receive to create a sense of urgency and FOMO (fear of missing out).

c) Free Resources or Tools: Offer free resources, templates, checklists, or tools that are valuable to your target audience. Position these resources as a practical solution to their pain points or challenges.

d) Contest Entries: Allow visitors to enter contests or giveaways by subscribing to your email list. Highlight attractive prizes and emphasize the excitement and opportunity to win.

e) Personalization and Customization: Tailor the opt-in incentives based on the specific interests and preferences of the visitor. For example, if they were browsing specific product categories, offer personalized recommendations or discounts related to those categories.

By implementing exit intent pop-ups, designing effective visuals and copy, and offering irresistible opt-in incentives, you can effectively capture visitors who are about to leave your website and convert them into valuable email subscribers.

Chapter 19: Leveraging the Power of Referrals

Referrals are a powerful and cost-effective way to grow your email list. By encouraging your existing subscribers to refer others, you can tap into their networks and attract new, highly engaged subscribers. In this chapter, we will explore the leverage of referrals for list growth, creating a referral program, incentivizing subscribers to refer others, and effectively tracking and rewarding referrals.

19.1 Creating a Referral Program for List Growth

A referral program provides a structured framework for your subscribers to refer others and actively contribute to the growth of your email list. Here are the key steps to create a referral program:

a) Set Clear Goals: Define your objectives for the referral program. Determine how many new subscribers you aim to acquire through referrals and the timeframe for achieving your goals.

b) Define Incentives: Determine the incentives you will offer to subscribers who refer others. These incentives can include exclusive content, discounts, special offers, or even rewards like gift cards or entry into contests.

c) Establish Program Guidelines: Clearly outline the guidelines and rules of your referral program. Specify how referrals should be made, any eligibility criteria, and the process for tracking and rewarding successful referrals.

d) Promote the Referral Program: Spread the word about your referral program through various channels, such as your website, email newsletters, social media, and blog posts. Highlight the benefits of participating and encourage subscribers to refer their friends and colleagues.

19.2 Incentivizing Subscribers to Refer Others

To encourage your subscribers to refer others, it's essential to offer enticing incentives and make it worth their while. Consider these strategies to incentivize subscribers to refer others:

a) Exclusive Benefits: Offer exclusive benefits or rewards to subscribers who refer others. This could be early access to new content, VIP treatment, or additional perks that are not available to regular subscribers.

b) Tiered Rewards: Implement a tiered reward system where subscribers receive increasing rewards for multiple successful referrals. This can motivate them to refer more people and strive for higher rewards.

c) Mutual Benefits: Structure the referral program in a way that provides benefits to both the referrer and the referred person. For example, offer a discount or bonus to both parties when a successful referral is made.

d) Social Recognition: Provide social recognition to subscribers who refer others by featuring them on your website or social media platforms. Publicly acknowledge their contribution and highlight their success in growing your community.

19.3 Tracking and Rewarding Referrals

Effectively tracking and rewarding referrals is crucial for the success of your referral program. Here's how you can ensure accurate tracking and provide appropriate rewards:

a) Unique Referral Links: Provide each subscriber with a unique referral link that they can share with their contacts. This allows you to track the source of each referral and attribute it to the respective subscriber.

b) Analytics and Reporting: Utilize analytics tools or referral tracking software to monitor the performance of your referral program. Track the number of referrals, conversion rates, and the overall impact on list growth.

c) Automated Reward System: Implement an automated system that tracks successful referrals and automatically delivers the rewards to both the referrer and the referred person. This ensures a seamless and efficient process.

d) Personalized Thank-You Messages: Send personalized thank-you messages to subscribers who successfully refer others. Show your appreciation for their contribution and make them feel valued as advocates for your brand.

e) Ongoing Engagement: Continue engaging with the referred subscribers to nurture their relationship with your brand. Provide them with valuable content, exclusive offers, and incentives to remain active and become loyal subscribers.

By leveraging the power of referrals, creating a referral program, incentivizing subscribers to refer others, and effectively tracking and rewarding referrals, you can harness the network effect to exponentially grow your email list.

Chapter 20: Using Quizzes and Assessments

Quizzes and assessments are powerful tools for engaging your audience, collecting email addresses, and tailoring follow-up content based on individual preferences and interests. In this chapter, we will explore the utilization of quizzes and assessments to enhance your list building efforts. We will delve into creating engaging quizzes and assessments, collecting email addresses through these interactive experiences, and tailoring follow-up content to provide personalized value.

20.1 Creating Engaging Quizzes and Assessments

Creating engaging quizzes and assessments involves crafting compelling questions and providing valuable results that resonate with your target audience. Here are some steps to create captivating quizzes and assessments:

a) Define the Purpose: Determine the objective of your quiz or assessment. Is it to educate, entertain, or provide insights? Clarifying your purpose will guide the design and content creation process.

b) Choose the Right Format: Select the format that best suits your goals and audience. This could include multiple-choice questions, personality assessments, knowledge tests, or interactive surveys.

c) Craft Relevant and Engaging Questions: Develop questions that are relevant to your audience's interests, pain points, or preferences. Make them intriguing, thought-provoking, and align them with the outcome you want to achieve.

d) Provide Meaningful Results: Ensure that the quiz or assessment delivers valuable and personalized results to participants. The outcome should provide insights, recommendations, or actionable steps related to their specific situation or interests.

e) Incorporate Visuals and Interactive Elements: Use visuals, images, videos, and interactive elements to enhance the engagement and appeal of the quiz or assessment. Visuals can capture attention and make the experience more enjoyable.

20.2 Collecting Email Addresses through Quizzes

Quizzes and assessments offer an excellent opportunity to collect email addresses from participants who are already engaged with your content. Here are some effective strategies to collect email addresses through quizzes:

a) Opt-In Form Integration: Integrate an opt-in form into your quiz or assessment, strategically placed before or after the quiz experience. Request participants' email addresses in exchange for receiving their quiz results or additional content.

b) Incentivize Participation: Offer an incentive for participants to provide their email addresses, such as exclusive access to bonus content, discounts, or entry into a giveaway. Clearly communicate the value they will receive by subscribing.

c) Progressive Profiling: Utilize progressive profiling to collect additional information beyond just the email address. Ask for more details as participants progress through the quiz, gradually building a richer profile of each subscriber.

d) Permission-Based Opt-In: Ensure that participants explicitly opt-in to receive future communications from you. Provide a checkbox or consent statement that clearly outlines the type of content they will receive and how frequently.

20.3 Tailoring Follow-up Content Based on Results

Once participants have completed the quiz or assessment, it's crucial to tailor the follow-up content to provide a personalized experience. Consider these strategies:

a) Results Email: Send a personalized email with the quiz results, highlighting the key insights or recommendations based on their responses. Make the email visually appealing and easy to understand, reinforcing the value of their participation.

b) Segmented Email Campaigns: Segment your email list based on quiz results or outcomes. Craft targeted email campaigns that provide relevant content, resources, or offers based on each subscriber's specific interests or preferences.

c) Content Recommendations: Recommend specific blog posts, articles, videos, or resources that align with the participant's quiz results. This demonstrates your understanding of their needs and provides further value.

d) Personalized Calls-to-Action: Include personalized calls-to-action in your emails that prompt subscribers to take specific actions related to their quiz results. This could be signing up for a webinar, downloading a guide, or making a purchase.

e) Nurture and Engagement: Continue nurturing the relationship with quiz participants by providing ongoing valuable content, updates, and exclusive offers tailored to their interests. Maintain regular communication to keep them engaged and connected to your brand.

By utilizing quizzes and assessments, collecting email addresses through these interactive experiences, and tailoring follow-up content based on individual results, you can create personalized experiences that drive engagement and list growth.

Chapter 21: Engaging Subscribers with Interactive Content

Interactive content has become a cornerstone of modern digital marketing, offering an immersive and engaging experience for subscribers. In this chapter, we will explore various interactive content formats, discuss how to incorporate interactive elements into emails, and unveil strategies for boosting engagement and list growth.

21.1 Exploring Interactive Content Formats

Interactive content takes many forms, each with its unique appeal. Here are some popular interactive content formats:

a) Quizzes and Assessments:

Engage your audience with quizzes or assessments that provide personalized results.

Collect valuable data while offering an entertaining experience.

b) Polls and Surveys:

Foster engagement by seeking opinions or feedback through polls and surveys.

Use insights to tailor your content strategy and improve user experience.

c) Calculators and Tools:

Offer interactive calculators or tools that help users solve problems or make informed decisions.

Collect user data and position your brand as a valuable resource.

d) Interactive Infographics:

Transform static information into interactive visuals that allow users to explore content dynamically.

Enhance the learning experience and encourage social sharing.

e) 360-Degree Videos and Virtual Tours:

Provide immersive experiences with 360-degree videos or virtual tours.

Showcase products, services, or behind-the-scenes views to captivate your audience.

21.2 Incorporating Interactive Elements in Emails

Incorporating interactive elements into your email campaigns can significantly enhance engagement. Here's how to do it effectively:

a) Animated GIFs:

Use animated GIFs to add movement and capture attention.

Showcase product features, highlight promotions, or tell a short story.

b) Interactive Images:

Embed images with clickable hotspots that lead to additional content.

Enhance product showcases or provide more information about specific elements.

c) Interactive Forms:

Include interactive forms directly in emails for feedback or sign-ups.

Reduce friction by allowing users to take action without leaving their inbox.

d) Countdown Timers:

Create a sense of urgency with countdown timers for limited-time offers.

Encourage subscribers to act promptly to avail themselves of special promotions.

21.3 Boosting Engagement and List Growth

Engaging subscribers with interactive content goes beyond the immediate interaction. Here are strategies to boost engagement and list growth:

a) Personalization:

Leverage user responses from interactive content to personalize future communications.

Tailor email campaigns based on quiz results, survey responses, or interactive tool usage.

b) Incentives and Rewards:

Encourage participation in interactive content with incentives.

Offer exclusive discounts, early access, or special content to those who engage.

c) Social Sharing:

Integrate features that enable users to share their interactive experiences on social media.

Leverage user-generated content to expand your reach and attract new subscribers.

d) Follow-up Campaigns:

Design follow-up email campaigns that build on the interactive experience.

Provide additional insights, resources, or exclusive offers related to the user's interaction.

e) Segmentation:

Use interactive content data to segment your email list.

Send targeted content to specific segments based on their preferences and interactions.

f) Continuous Innovation:

Stay ahead by continually innovating your interactive content.

Introduce new quizzes, tools, or experiences to keep subscribers engaged and looking forward to your emails.

By exploring diverse interactive content formats, incorporating interactive elements in emails, and implementing strategies for engagement and list growth, you can create a dynamic and compelling experience for your subscribers.

Chapter 22: Leveraging User-generated Content

User-generated content (UGC) has emerged as a powerful tool for marketers to engage their audience, foster authenticity, and build a sense of community around their brand. In this chapter, we will explore the strategies for leveraging user-generated content effectively, from encouraging subscribers to contribute content to showcasing it in emails and building a thriving community around it.

22.1 Encouraging Subscribers to Contribute Content

Encouraging subscribers to contribute content involves creating opportunities for them to share their experiences, opinions, and creativity. Here are some effective strategies for encouraging user-generated content:

Firstly, create dedicated spaces or platforms where subscribers can submit their content, such as social media channels, online forums, or branded hashtags. Encourage participation by highlighting user contributions and acknowledging their efforts publicly.

Secondly, incentivize content creation by offering rewards, recognition, or exclusive privileges to contributors. This could include featuring their content in email campaigns, granting access to exclusive events or content, or providing discounts or freebies.

Thirdly, engage with your audience proactively by initiating conversations, asking for feedback, and responding to user-generated content promptly and authentically. Show appreciation for their contributions and foster a sense of belonging within your community.

22.2 Showcasing User-generated Content in Emails

Showcasing user-generated content in emails allows you to leverage social proof, foster engagement, and provide valuable insights to your subscribers. Here are some effective ways to showcase user-generated content in emails:

Firstly, curate user-generated content that aligns with your brand's messaging and values. Select compelling examples that showcase diverse perspectives, experiences, and creativity.

Secondly, incorporate user-generated content strategically within your email campaigns. This could include featuring user testimonials, reviews, photos, or stories that highlight the benefits of your products or services.

Thirdly, personalize the user-generated content experience by segmenting your email list based on subscriber preferences and interests. Tailor the content to resonate with specific audience segments and increase relevance and engagement.

22.3 Building a Community Around User-generated Content

Building a community around user-generated content involves fostering meaningful connections, facilitating interactions, and creating a sense of belonging among your audience. Here are some strategies for building a thriving community around user-generated content:

Firstly, provide opportunities for collaboration and co-creation by inviting subscribers to participate in contests, challenges, or collaborative projects. Encourage peer-to-peer interactions and celebrate the contributions of community members.

Secondly, cultivate a supportive and inclusive environment where subscribers feel empowered to share their experiences, ideas, and feedback openly. Implement community guidelines and moderation strategies to maintain a positive and respectful atmosphere.

Thirdly, foster engagement by organizing virtual events, webinars, or meetups where subscribers can connect with each other and with your brand. Create spaces for discussions, networking, and knowledge sharing.

By leveraging user-generated content, showcasing it in emails, and building a community around it, you can harness the power of your audience to create authentic, engaging experiences that drive brand loyalty and advocacy.

Chapter 23: Collaborating with Strategic Partners

Collaborating with strategic partners can be a game-changer for expanding your reach, accessing new audiences, and driving mutual growth. In this chapter, we will delve into the strategies for collaborating with strategic partners effectively, from identifying potential partners to implementing co-branded campaigns and cross-promoting to expand reach.

23.1 Identifying Potential Strategic Partners

Identifying potential strategic partners involves finding organizations or individuals whose audience, values, and goals align with yours. Here are some key steps for identifying potential strategic partners:

Firstly, conduct market research to identify organizations or individuals operating in complementary or related niches. Look for partners whose products, services, or content resonate with your target audience.

Secondly, analyze the audience demographics, size, and engagement of potential partners to ensure alignment with your target market. Evaluate their online presence, social media following, and reputation within their industry.

Thirdly, consider the potential for mutual benefit and value exchange in the partnership. Look for partners who can offer unique expertise, resources, or promotional opportunities that complement your own offerings.

23.2 Implementing Co-branded Campaigns

Implementing co-branded campaigns involves collaborating with strategic partners to create joint marketing initiatives that leverage each other's brand and audience. Here are some steps for implementing co-branded campaigns successfully:

Firstly, define clear objectives and goals for the co-branded campaign, outlining what you aim to achieve and how success will be measured. Align on key performance indicators (KPIs) and expectations with your partner.

Secondly, develop a co-branded campaign strategy that highlights the unique value proposition of the partnership and resonates with both audiences. Create compelling messaging and visuals that showcase the combined benefits of your offerings.

Thirdly, allocate roles and responsibilities between you and your partner, ensuring clear communication and coordination throughout the campaign. Establish timelines, deadlines, and checkpoints to keep the campaign on track.

23.3 Cross-Promoting to Expand Reach

Cross-promoting with strategic partners involves leveraging each other's channels, platforms, and audiences to amplify reach and engagement. Here are some strategies for cross-promoting effectively:

Firstly, collaborate on content creation and distribution, such as guest blogging, co-hosting webinars, or creating joint social media campaigns. Share each other's content with your respective audiences to increase visibility and credibility.

Secondly, leverage email marketing to reach each other's subscribers with targeted promotions, offers, or content recommendations. Coordinate email campaigns to coincide with key milestones or events.

Thirdly, explore opportunities for offline collaboration, such as hosting joint events, sponsoring conferences, or participating in industry trade shows. Capitalize on face-to-face interactions to deepen relationships and foster trust with   both   audiences.

By collaborating with strategic partners, implementing co-branded campaigns, and cross-promoting to expand reach, you can tap into new markets, amplify your message, and drive mutual growth. Choose partners wisely, align on objectives, and leverage each other's strengths to create impactful collaborations.

Chapter 24: Hosting Virtual Events for List Building

Hosting virtual events presents an invaluable opportunity to engage with your audience, establish authority in your niche, and significantly grow your email list. In this chapter, we'll explore the different types of virtual events you can host for effective list building, including organizing virtual conferences or summits, hosting webinars and workshops, and collecting leads during virtual events.

Organizing Virtual Conferences or Summits (24.1)
Virtual conferences or summits offer a comprehensive platform to showcase expertise, facilitate networking, and attract a wide range of attendees. Here's how you can effectively organize virtual conferences or summits for list building:

Select a Theme: Choose a compelling theme or topic that resonates with your target audience and aligns with your expertise. Ensure that the theme has broad appeal and can attract a diverse audience.

Curate Speakers: Invite industry experts, thought leaders, and influencers to speak at your virtual conference or summit. Curate a lineup of speakers who can provide valuable insights, engage the audience, and attract attendees.

Promote Registration: Create a dedicated landing page for your virtual event and promote registration across various channels, including email, social media, and partner networks. Offer early bird discounts or incentives to encourage early sign-ups.

Deliver Engaging Content: Plan a diverse range of sessions, panels, workshops, and networking opportunities to keep attendees engaged throughout the event. Incorporate interactive elements such as Q&A sessions, polls, and breakout discussions to foster participation.

Hosting Webinars and Workshops (24.2)
Webinars and workshops are highly effective for providing in-depth insights, facilitating interaction, and capturing leads. Here's how you can host engaging webinars and workshops for list building:

Choose Relevant Topics: Select topics that address the pain points, challenges, or interests of your target audience. Focus on providing actionable insights, practical tips, and valuable takeaways that attendees can apply immediately.

Promote Registration: Promote your webinars and workshops through email invitations, social media posts, and website announcements. Highlight the benefits of attending and emphasize the value of the content you'll be covering.

Create Compelling Content: Develop engaging presentations, demonstrations, or case studies to deliver during your webinar or workshop. Use visuals, storytelling, and real-life examples to make the content relatable and memorable.

Capture Leads: Use registration forms or lead capture tools to collect attendee information, including names, email addresses, and any additional details you require. Follow up with attendees after the event to nurture leads and continue the conversation.

Collecting Leads during Virtual Events (24.3)

Collecting leads during virtual events is essential for growing your email list and nurturing relationships with attendees. Here are some strategies for effectively collecting leads during virtual events:

Use Registration Forms: Require attendees to provide their contact information when registering for your virtual event. Include fields for names, email addresses, company names, and any other relevant details you need for segmentation.

Engage with Attendees: Encourage interaction and engagement during your virtual event by incorporating live chat, polls, and Q&A sessions. Use these opportunities to gather additional insights about attendees and their interests.

Offer Incentives: Provide incentives for attendees to share their contact information, such as exclusive resources, downloadable content, or entry into a prize draw. Highlight the value of subscribing to your email list and staying connected.

Follow Up Promptly: After the virtual event, follow up promptly with attendees to thank them for participating and provide additional resources or information. Use automated email sequences to nurture leads and encourage further engagement.

By organizing virtual conferences or summits, hosting webinars and workshops, and collecting leads during virtual events, you can effectively grow your email list and cultivate relationships with your audience. Focus on delivering valuable content, engaging attendees, and providing opportunities for interaction and follow-up.

Chapter 25: Leveraging Offline Channels for List Building

In today's digital age, offline channels still hold significant potential for expanding your email list and reaching new audiences. In this chapter, we'll explore how you can leverage offline channels effectively for list building, including collecting email addresses at events or trade shows, using direct mail to drive online subscriptions, and utilizing print advertising for list growth.

25.1 Collecting Email Addresses at Events or Trade Shows
Events and trade shows provide valuable opportunities to connect with potential subscribers in person and collect their email addresses. Here's how you can effectively collect email addresses at events or trade shows:

Use Lead Capture Tools: Utilize lead capture tools such as tablets or mobile devices equipped with forms to collect attendee information. Offer incentives such as exclusive content or giveaways to encourage sign-ups.

Offer Onsite Registration: Set up registration booths or kiosks where attendees can sign up for your email list onsite. Make the process quick and convenient, and ensure that staff are available to assist and answer questions.

Host Contests or Giveaways: Host contests or giveaways at your booth to attract attendees and incentivize email sign-ups. Require participants to provide their email addresses for entry into the contest or to receive the giveaway.

25.2 Using Direct Mail to Drive Online Subscriptions

Direct mail remains a powerful marketing tool for reaching targeted audiences and driving online subscriptions. Here's how you can use direct mail to drive online subscriptions:

Include Call-to-Action Cards: Include call-to-action (CTA) cards in your direct mail pieces that prompt recipients to visit your website and subscribe to your email list. Offer a compelling reason for them to subscribe, such as access to exclusive content or special offers.

Offer QR Codes or Short URLs: Include QR codes or short URLs in your direct mail pieces that recipients can scan or type into their browser to easily access your subscription page. Make it as simple as possible for them to subscribe online.

Personalize Your Messaging: Personalize your direct mail messaging to resonate with recipients and encourage them to take action. Tailor your messaging to their interests, preferences, or previous interactions with your brand to increase relevance and engagement.

25.3 Utilizing Print Advertising for List Growth

Print advertising in newspapers, magazines, or other publications can effectively reach your target audience and drive list growth. Here's how you can utilize print advertising for list growth:

Include Email Sign-Up Forms: Include email sign-up forms or QR codes in your print advertisements that direct readers to your subscription page. Offer an incentive or exclusive offer to encourage them to subscribe.

Run Contests or Promotions: Run contests or promotions in print publications that require readers to provide their email addresses for entry. Highlight the benefits of subscribing to your email list and make it easy for them to sign up.

Track and Measure Results: Track and measure the effectiveness of your print advertising campaigns in driving email sign-ups. Monitor metrics such as response rates, conversion rates, and subscriber growth to assess the impact of your efforts.

By leveraging offline channels such as events or trade shows, direct mail, and print advertising for list building, you can reach new audiences and expand your email list in meaningful ways. Focus on providing value, making it easy for recipients to subscribe, and tracking the results of your efforts to optimize your list-building strategies over time.

Chapter 26: Creating a Sense of Urgency and Scarcity

In marketing, creating a sense of urgency and scarcity can compel potential subscribers to take action promptly, leading to increased sign-ups and conversions. In this chapter, we'll explore effective strategies for leveraging urgency and scarcity to drive email list growth and boost conversions.

26.1 Using Limited-Time Offers to Drive Sign-ups

Limited-time offers are a powerful way to create urgency and incentivize sign-ups to your email list. Here's how you can use them effectively:

Offer Time-Limited Discounts: Provide exclusive discounts or promotions to new subscribers for a limited time only. Highlight the savings and emphasize that the offer will expire soon to encourage immediate action.

Promote Limited-Time Freebies: Offer freebies, such as e-books, guides, or templates, to new subscribers for a limited time. Clearly communicate that the freebie is only available for a short period, motivating visitors to subscribe before it's too late.

Run Flash Sales: Host flash sales or special events where subscribers can access discounted products or services for a brief window of time. Create a sense of urgency by promoting the limited duration of the sale and the scarcity of the deals.

26.2 Implementing Countdown Timers and Exclusivity

Countdown timers and exclusivity can add an extra layer of urgency and scarcity to your email list building efforts. Here's how you can implement them effectively:

Use Countdown Timers: Incorporate countdown timers into your website, landing pages, or email campaigns to visually highlight the limited time remaining for special offers or promotions. Countdown timers create a sense of urgency and encourage immediate action.

Offer Exclusive Access: Provide exclusive access or early bird benefits to subscribers who sign up within a specified timeframe. Communicate the exclusivity of the offer and the benefits of being among the first to join your email list to drive sign-ups.

Create Limited-Spots Offers: Limit the availability of certain offers or promotions to a specific number of spots or seats. Communicate the scarcity of the offer and encourage subscribers to act quickly to secure their spot before they run out.

26.3 Leveraging Urgency and Scarcity to Increase Conversions

Urgency and scarcity can significantly increase conversions by motivating subscribers to take immediate action. Here's how you can leverage them to boost conversions:

Use Compelling Copy: Craft persuasive copy that communicates the urgency and scarcity of your offers effectively. Use phrases such as "limited time only," "act now," or "while supplies last" to convey the time-sensitive nature of the offer.

Create FOMO (Fear of Missing Out): Tap into the fear of missing out (FOMO) by highlighting the potential loss or regret of not taking advantage of the offer. Use social proof, testimonials, or real-time notifications to reinforce the popularity and desirability of the offer.

Optimize Call-to-Action (CTA): Optimize your call-to-action (CTA) buttons and copy to align with the sense of urgency and scarcity. Use action-oriented language and visually compelling buttons that prompt subscribers to take immediate action.

By effectively using limited-time offers, countdown timers, exclusivity, and persuasive copy, you can create a sense of urgency and scarcity that drives sign-ups to your email list and increases conversions. Experiment with different tactics and monitor the results to optimize your list-building strategies over time.

Chapter 27: Implementing Exit-Intent Surveys

Exit-intent surveys are a valuable tool for capturing feedback from visitors who are about to leave your website. By understanding their concerns and motivations, you can identify conversion barriers, make improvements, and optimize the user experience to drive list growth. In this chapter, we'll explore how to effectively implement exit-intent surveys to gather feedback and enhance your email list building efforts.

27.1 Capturing Feedback with Exit-Intent Surveys

Exit-intent surveys allow you to capture valuable feedback from visitors who are on the verge of leaving your website. Here's how you can effectively capture feedback with exit-intent surveys:

Strategically Time the Survey: Set up the exit-intent survey to trigger when a visitor's mouse cursor moves towards the browser's navigation bar or close button, indicating an intent to leave the page. This timing ensures that you capture feedback from visitors who may have encountered obstacles or concerns during their visit.

Ask Relevant Questions: Keep your exit-intent survey concise and focused on gathering actionable insights. Ask questions that help you understand visitors' reasons for leaving, such as "What prevented you from completing your purchase?" or "Is there anything we could improve to better meet your needs?"

Offer Incentives: Encourage visitors to participate in the exit-intent survey by offering incentives such as discounts, freebies, or entry into a prize draw. Highlight the value of their feedback and how it will help improve their experience in the future.

27.2 Identifying Conversion Barriers and Improvements

Exit-intent surveys provide valuable insights into the conversion barriers and areas for improvement on your website. Here's how you can effectively identify conversion barriers and make improvements based on the feedback gathered:

Analyze Survey Responses: Review the responses collected from the exit-intent survey to identify common themes, pain points, and areas of friction experienced by visitors. Look for patterns or trends that indicate potential conversion barriers or usability issues.

Address Common Concerns: Take action to address the common concerns or objections raised by visitors in the exit-intent survey. This may involve making changes to your website's design, navigation, checkout process, or product offerings to alleviate barriers to conversion.

Test and Iterate: Implement changes based on the feedback gathered from exit-intent surveys and monitor their impact on conversion rates and user satisfaction. Continuously test and iterate on your website to optimize the user experience and address any remaining conversion barriers.

27.3 Optimizing the User Experience for List Growth

Optimizing the user experience based on insights from exit-intent surveys can drive list growth by improving visitor satisfaction and conversion rates. Here's how you can optimize the user experience for list growth:

Streamline Sign-Up Process: Simplify the sign-up process for your email list by reducing form fields, offering social login options, or implementing one-click sign-ups. Make it as easy and frictionless as possible for visitors to subscribe to your email list.

Offer Personalized Recommendations: Use insights from exit-intent surveys to personalize the user experience and provide relevant recommendations or content based on visitors' preferences and interests. Tailor your messaging and offers to resonate with their needs and motivations.

Provide Value-Added Incentives: Offer value-added incentives such as exclusive content, discounts, or early access to encourage visitors to subscribe to your email list. Highlight the benefits of subscribing and how it will enhance their experience with your brand.

By effectively implementing exit-intent surveys, capturing feedback, identifying conversion barriers, and optimizing the user experience for list growth, you can enhance visitor satisfaction, drive conversions, and grow your email list effectively. Continuously gather feedback, make improvements, and iterate on your strategies to maximize results over time.

Chapter 28: Leveraging Customer Testimonials

Customer testimonials are a powerful tool for building trust, credibility, and social proof for your brand. In this chapter, we'll explore how you can effectively leverage customer testimonials to enhance your email list building efforts.

28.1 Collecting and Showcasing Customer Testimonials

Collecting and showcasing customer testimonials involves gathering feedback from satisfied customers and displaying it prominently to prospective subscribers. Here's how you can effectively collect and showcase customer testimonials:

Solicit Feedback: Reach out to satisfied customers and request their feedback on their experience with your products or services. Use surveys, email follow-ups, or dedicated feedback forms to collect testimonials.

Diversify Testimonials: Gather testimonials from a diverse range of customers, including different demographics, industries, or use cases. This ensures that your testimonials resonate with a broader audience and address various pain points or objections.

Display Prominently: Showcase customer testimonials prominently on your website, landing pages, and email campaigns. Use compelling visuals, such as photos or videos, to make testimonials more impactful and engaging.

28.2 Using Testimonials to Build Trust and Credibility

Customer testimonials are instrumental in building trust and credibility with prospective subscribers. Here's how you can leverage testimonials to build trust and credibility:

Highlight Success Stories: Use customer testimonials to highlight success stories, case studies, or specific results achieved by customers using your products or services. Provide concrete examples of how your offerings have helped customers solve their problems or achieve their goals.

Feature Real People: Ensure that your testimonials feature real people with authentic experiences. Include their names, photos, or even video testimonials to make them more relatable and credible.

Address Objections: Use testimonials to address common objections or concerns that prospective subscribers may have. Highlight how your products or services have overcome challenges or exceeded expectations for previous customers.

28.3 Incorporating Testimonials in Opt-In Processes

Incorporating testimonials into your opt-in processes can significantly enhance their effectiveness in persuading visitors to subscribe to your email list. Here's how you can incorporate testimonials into opt-in processes:

Include Social Proof: Display customer testimonials near your opt-in forms or calls-to-action to provide social proof and reinforce the value of subscribing. Use persuasive copy that emphasizes the benefits of joining your email list.

Use Testimonial CTAs: Create call-to-action buttons or links that feature customer testimonials alongside the opt-in form. For example, "Join thousands of satisfied customers and subscribe to our newsletter today!"

Showcase Subscriber Benefits: Use testimonials to highlight the benefits that subscribers will receive by joining your email list. For example, "Read what our subscribers are saying about our exclusive content and special offers!"

By effectively collecting and showcasing customer testimonials, using them to build trust and credibility, and incorporating them into your opt-in processes, you can enhance your email list building efforts and attract more subscribers. Testimonials provide valuable social proof and demonstrate the value of subscribing to your email list, making them a valuable asset in your marketing toolkit.

Chapter 29: Implementing Lead Scoring

Lead scoring is a crucial component of effective email list management, allowing you to prioritize and focus your efforts on leads most likely to convert into customers. In this chapter, we'll delve into the importance of lead scoring, how to assign values to subscriber actions, and strategies for segmenting and prioritizing leads for maximum return on investment.

29.1 Understanding the Importance of Lead Scoring

Lead scoring is essential for identifying and prioritizing leads based on their likelihood to convert. By assigning scores to leads based on their engagement, demographics, and behavior, you can focus your resources on high-value prospects and improve conversion rates. Understanding the importance of lead scoring allows you to:

Prioritize Resources: Allocate your time, budget, and efforts more efficiently by focusing on leads with the highest likelihood of conversion.

Improve Sales Efficiency: Provide your sales team with qualified leads that are more likely to convert, allowing them to prioritize their efforts and close deals more effectively.

Enhance Personalization: Tailor your marketing messages and campaigns to the specific needs and interests of different lead segments, improving engagement and conversion rates.

29.2 Assigning Values to Subscriber Actions

Assigning values to subscriber actions involves quantifying the impact of various interactions and behaviors on lead quality and conversion likelihood. Here's how you can assign values to subscriber actions effectively:

Define Scoring Criteria: Identify key actions and behaviors that indicate lead engagement and interest, such as email opens, clicks, website visits, content downloads, and webinar attendance.

Assign Point Values: Assign point values to each action based on its significance and impact on lead quality. For example, a webinar attendance may be assigned a higher score than a simple email open.

Track and Accumulate Scores: Track and accumulate scores for individual leads based on their interactions over time. Regularly update and adjust scoring criteria as needed to reflect changes in lead behavior and engagement.

29.3 Segmenting and Prioritizing Leads for Maximum ROI

Segmenting and prioritizing leads based on lead scores allows you to tailor your marketing efforts and messaging to different lead segments effectively. Here's how you can segment and prioritize leads for maximum return on investment:

Create Lead Segments: Segment leads into different categories based on their lead scores, demographics, interests, and behaviors. Common segments may include hot leads, warm leads, and cold leads.

Prioritize Follow-Up: Prioritize follow-up and engagement efforts based on lead scores, focusing on high-scoring leads with the greatest potential for conversion. Tailor your messaging and offers to each segment's needs and interests.

Automate Lead Nurturing: Implement automated lead nurturing workflows based on lead scores, delivering targeted content and communications to leads at different stages of the buyer's journey. Use lead scores to trigger specific actions and communications.

By implementing lead scoring, assigning values to subscriber actions, and segmenting and prioritizing leads effectively, you can optimize your email list management efforts and improve conversion rates. Lead scoring allows you to focus your resources on high-value prospects, enhance personalization, and maximize return on investment from your email marketing efforts.

Chapter 30: Building Relationships through Email Nurture Campaigns

Email nurture campaigns are a powerful tool for building relationships, providing value, and ultimately converting subscribers into loyal customers. In this chapter, we'll explore how to create engaging email nurture sequences, provide value, and build trust over time, ultimately leading to conversions and customer loyalty.

30.1 Creating Engaging Email Nurture Sequences

Creating engaging email nurture sequences involves delivering relevant, personalized content to subscribers at different stages of the buyer's journey. Here's how you can create effective email nurture sequences:

Segment Your Audience: Segment your email list based on subscriber interests, demographics, and behaviors to deliver targeted content that resonates with each segment.

Map Out the Buyer's Journey: Identify the different stages of the buyer's journey, from awareness to consideration to decision, and develop email content that guides subscribers through each stage.

Deliver Value at Every Touchpoint: Provide valuable, educational content that addresses subscriber pain points, challenges, and goals. Use a mix of educational content, product information, testimonials, and offers to keep subscribers engaged and moving through the buyer's journey.

30.2 Providing Value and Building Trust over Time

Providing value and building trust over time is essential for nurturing relationships with subscribers and establishing credibility. Here's how you can provide value and build trust through email nurture campaigns:

Educate and Inform: Offer valuable insights, tips, and resources that help subscribers solve problems, achieve goals, or improve their lives in some way. Position yourself as a trusted advisor and expert in your industry.

Personalize Your Content: Tailor your email content to the specific interests, preferences, and behaviors of individual subscribers. Use personalization techniques such as dynamic content, segmentation, and triggered emails to deliver relevant content that resonates with each subscriber.

Be Consistent and Reliable: Maintain a consistent sending schedule and deliver high-quality content consistently over time. Build trust with subscribers by demonstrating reliability, professionalism, and authenticity in your communications.

30.3 Converting Subscribers into Loyal Customers

Converting subscribers into loyal customers is the ultimate goal of email nurture campaigns. Here's how you can effectively convert subscribers into loyal customers:

Nurture Relationships: Continue to nurture relationships with subscribers even after they become customers. Provide ongoing value, support, and personalized recommendations to deepen their loyalty and engagement with your brand.

Promote Customer Loyalty Programs: Encourage customers to join your loyalty program and reward them for their continued engagement and purchases. Offer exclusive perks, discounts, and rewards to incentivize repeat business and foster loyalty.

Ask for Feedback and Reviews: Solicit feedback and reviews from customers to gather valuable insights and testimonials that can be used to improve your products, services, and customer experience. Use positive reviews and testimonials to reinforce trust and credibility with potential customers.

By creating engaging email nurture sequences, providing value, building trust over time, and ultimately converting subscribers into loyal customers, you can maximize the effectiveness of your email marketing efforts and drive long-term success for your business. Focus on building authentic relationships, delivering value, and exceeding customer expectations to foster loyalty and retention over time.

Chapter 31: Leveraging Influencer Partnerships

Influencer partnerships offer a valuable opportunity to expand your reach, build credibility, and drive list growth through endorsements from trusted voices in your industry. In this chapter, we'll explore how to effectively leverage influencer partnerships to grow your email list.

31.1 Identifying and Engaging with Industry Influencers
Identifying and engaging with industry influencers is the first step in leveraging influencer partnerships for list building. Here's how you can identify and engage with influencers effectively:

Research Relevant Influencers: Identify influencers in your niche who have a significant following and influence over your target audience. Look for influencers who align with your brand values and have a genuine connection with their followers.

Engage with Influencers: Build relationships with influencers by following them on social media, engaging with their content, and sharing their posts. Show genuine interest in their work and offer value before reaching out with partnership proposals.

Reach Out with Personalized Pitches: Craft personalized pitches that demonstrate your understanding of the influencer's audience and how your partnership can provide value to their followers. Highlight the benefits of collaborating with your brand and how it aligns with their interests and goals.

31.2 Collaborating with Influencers for List Building
Collaborating with influencers for list building involves leveraging their influence to promote your email list and attract new subscribers. Here's how you can collaborate with influencers effectively:

Co-create Valuable Content: Collaborate with influencers to create valuable content that resonates with their audience and encourages them to join your email list. This could include guest blog posts, social media takeovers, or co-hosted webinars or events.

Offer Exclusive Incentives: Provide influencers with exclusive incentives to share with their followers, such as discounts, giveaways, or access to premium content. Encourage influencers to promote your email list as a valuable resource for their audience.

Track and Attribute Sign-Ups: Use trackable links or unique promo codes to attribute sign-ups directly to influencer partnerships. Monitor the performance of influencer campaigns and adjust your approach based on the results.

31.3 Measuring the Success of Influencer Campaigns
Measuring the success of influencer campaigns is essential for evaluating their impact on list growth and ROI.

Here's how you can measure the success of influencer campaigns effectively:

Track Key Metrics: Monitor key metrics such as email sign-ups, click-through rates, conversions, and revenue generated from influencer partnerships. Use tracking tools and analytics to attribute results directly to influencer collaborations.

Assess Engagement and Reach: Evaluate the level of engagement and reach generated by influencer campaigns, including likes, shares, comments, and mentions. Analyze the sentiment and quality of interactions to gauge the effectiveness of influencer partnerships.

Calculate ROI: Calculate the return on investment (ROI) of influencer campaigns by comparing the cost of collaboration with the revenue generated from new subscribers and conversions. Consider both short-term and long-term impacts on list growth and customer acquisition.

By identifying and engaging with industry influencers, collaborating on valuable content and incentives for list building, and measuring the success of influencer campaigns, you can effectively leverage influencer partnerships to grow your email list and reach new audiences. Focus on building authentic relationships with influencers and providing value to their followers to maximize the impact of your partnerships over time.

Chapter 32: Maximizing Email Deliverability and Open Rates

Effective email deliverability and high open rates are crucial for the success of your email marketing efforts. In this chapter, we'll delve into the factors influencing email deliverability, best practices for inbox placement, and strategies to increase open rates through compelling subject lines.

32.1 Understanding Email Deliverability Factors

Email deliverability is influenced by various factors that determine whether your emails reach recipients' inboxes or end up in spam folders. Understanding these factors is essential for maximizing email deliverability. Key factors include:

Sender Reputation: Maintain a positive sender reputation by sending relevant, valuable content and avoiding spammy practices. Monitor your sender score and address any issues promptly to uphold a positive reputation.

Authentication Protocols: Implement authentication protocols such as SPF (Sender Policy Framework) and DKIM (DomainKeys Identified Mail) to verify your identity and prevent email spoofing. This helps build trust with email service providers (ESPs).

List Hygiene: Regularly clean and maintain your email list by removing inactive or bouncing subscribers. A clean list improves engagement metrics and signals to ESPs that your emails are wanted.

32.2 Implementing Best Practices for Inbox Placement

Inbox placement is the goal for maximizing the visibility of your emails. Implementing best practices ensures that your emails land in recipients' primary inboxes rather than being marked as spam. Key practices include:

Permission-Based Marketing: Only send emails to individuals who have explicitly opted in to receive them. Obtaining permission builds trust and reduces the likelihood of your emails being marked as spam.

Optimize Sending Frequency: Avoid sending too many emails in a short period, as this can trigger spam filters. Find the optimal sending frequency that maintains engagement without overwhelming subscribers.

Responsive Design: Ensure your emails are mobile-friendly and display well across different devices and email clients. Responsive design contributes to a positive user experience, which, in turn, affects inbox placement.

32.3 Increasing Open Rates through Compelling Subject Lines

Compelling subject lines are instrumental in grabbing subscribers' attention and increasing open rates. Here's how you can craft subject lines that entice recipients to open your emails:

Be Clear and Concise: Clearly communicate the value or content of the email in a concise manner. Avoid misleading or clickbait subject lines, as they can lead to decreased trust and engagement.

Personalization: Incorporate personalization elements such as the recipient's name to make the email feel more tailored and relevant to their interests.

Create a Sense of Urgency or Curiosity: Use language that creates a sense of urgency or curiosity to encourage recipients to open the email promptly. Limited-time offers or teasers can be effective in this regard.

Test and Optimize: A/B test different subject lines to identify which ones resonate best with your audience. Continuously analyze the performance of subject lines and optimize based on the results.

By understanding and actively managing email deliverability factors, implementing best practices for inbox placement, and crafting compelling subject lines, you can enhance the success of your email marketing campaigns. Regularly monitor key metrics, adapt to changes in subscriber behavior, and stay informed about industry trends to maintain a high level of engagement and open rates over time.

Chapter 33: Analyzing and Optimizing Email Campaigns

Analyzing and optimizing email campaigns is essential for maximizing their effectiveness and achieving your marketing goals. In this chapter, we'll explore how to track key email marketing metrics, analyze data to identify opportunities for improvement, and optimize campaigns for better results.

33.1 Tracking Key Email Marketing Metrics

Tracking key email marketing metrics provides valuable insights into the performance of your campaigns and subscriber engagement. Here are some essential metrics to track:

Open Rate: The percentage of recipients who open your email. A high open rate indicates strong subject lines and engaged subscribers.

Click-Through Rate (CTR): The percentage of recipients who click on links within your email. CTR measures the effectiveness of your content and calls-to-action.

Conversion Rate: The percentage of recipients who complete a desired action, such as making a purchase or filling out a form. Conversion rate indicates the overall effectiveness of your email campaign in driving desired outcomes.

Bounce Rate: The percentage of emails that are undeliverable due to invalid email addresses or other issues. High bounce rates can negatively impact sender reputation and deliverability.

Unsubscribe Rate: The percentage of recipients who unsubscribe from your email list after receiving a campaign. Monitoring unsubscribe rates helps gauge subscriber satisfaction and the relevance of your content.

33.2 Analyzing Data to Identify Opportunities for Improvement

Analyzing data allows you to identify trends, patterns, and areas for improvement in your email campaigns. Here's how you can analyze data effectively:

Segment Analysis: Compare the performance of different email segments to identify which segments are responding well to your campaigns and which may need adjustments.

Time and Day Analysis: Analyze the best times and days to send emails based on open and click-through rates. Optimize send times to maximize engagement and response rates.

Content Analysis: Evaluate the performance of different types of content, subject lines, and calls-to-action to determine what resonates best with your audience. Use A/B testing to experiment with variations and identify winning strategies.

33.3 Optimizing Campaigns for Better Results

Optimizing email campaigns involves making data-driven adjustments to improve performance and achieve better results. Here are some strategies for optimization:

Subject Line Optimization: Test different subject lines to determine which ones result in higher open rates. Experiment with personalization, urgency, and curiosity to capture recipients' attention.

Content Personalization: Use subscriber data to personalize email content, such as product recommendations, tailored offers, or personalized greetings. Personalized content fosters a stronger connection with subscribers and increases engagement.

Mobile Optimization: Ensure that your emails are mobile-friendly and display properly on various devices and screen sizes. Mobile optimization is essential for reaching subscribers who primarily access emails on smartphones or tablets.

Automation and Segmentation: Implement automated email workflows based on subscriber actions and preferences. Segment your email list to deliver targeted content that resonates with specific audience segments.

By tracking key email marketing metrics, analyzing data to identify opportunities for improvement, and optimizing campaigns based on insights, you can enhance the effectiveness of your email marketing efforts and achieve better results over time. Continuously monitor performance, experiment with different strategies, and iterate on your approach to stay ahead of the curve and maximize ROI.

Chapter 34: Implementing Retargeting Strategies

Retargeting strategies play a crucial role in re-engaging website visitors and converting them into subscribers. In this chapter, we'll explore how to effectively implement retargeting strategies to grow your email list.

34.1 Utilizing Website Retargeting for List Growth

Website retargeting involves targeting website visitors with ads after they leave your site, reminding them of your brand and encouraging them to take action. Here's how you can utilize website retargeting for list growth:

Set Up Retargeting Pixels: Install retargeting pixels on your website to track visitors' behavior and actions. Pixels allow you to create custom audiences of users who have visited specific pages or taken certain actions on your site.

Create Targeted Ads: Develop targeted ads that resonate with retargeted visitors and encourage them to join your email list. Highlight the benefits of subscribing and provide incentives such as discounts or exclusive content to entice sign-ups.

Optimize Landing Pages: Ensure that the landing pages you direct retargeted visitors to are optimized for conversions. Clear calls-to-action, compelling copy, and simple opt-in forms can help maximize sign-up rates.

34.2 Segmenting and Personalizing Retargeting Campaigns

Segmenting and personalizing retargeting campaigns allows you to tailor your messaging to different audience segments and increase relevance. Here's how you can implement segmentation and personalization:

Segment by Behavior: Segment retargeting audiences based on their behavior on your website, such as pages visited, products viewed, or actions taken. Tailor your retargeting ads and messaging to each segment's interests and preferences.

Personalize Ad Content: Use dynamic ad content to personalize retargeting ads based on users' past interactions with your site. Display relevant products, recommendations, or offers that align with their browsing history or previous purchases.

Test Different Variations: A/B test different ad creatives, messaging, and offers to identify the most effective combinations for driving conversions. Continuously monitor performance and optimize based on results.

34.3 Converting Lost Website Visitors into Subscribers
Converting lost website visitors into subscribers requires strategic messaging and compelling offers. Here's how you can effectively convert lost visitors into subscribers:

Offer Incentives: Provide incentives such as discounts, freebies, or exclusive content to encourage lost visitors to join your email list. Highlight the value they'll receive by subscribing and make the offer irresistible.

Use Urgency and Scarcity: Create a sense of urgency or scarcity in your retargeting ads and offers to prompt immediate action. Limited-time offers or exclusive deals can motivate lost visitors to take the next step and subscribe.

Follow Up with Email Campaigns: Once lost visitors have subscribed to your email list, follow up with targeted email campaigns to nurture the relationship and encourage further engagement. Provide valuable content and incentives to keep subscribers engaged and active.

By utilizing website retargeting, segmenting and personalizing retargeting campaigns, and effectively converting lost website visitors into subscribers, you can grow your email list and re-engage potential customers who have shown interest in your brand. Continuously refine your retargeting strategies based on performance data and audience feedback to maximize results over time.

Chapter 35: Leveraging Customer Referrals

Customer referrals are a powerful tool for growing your email list organically and acquiring high-quality subscribers. In this chapter, we'll explore how to effectively leverage customer referrals to expand your email list.

35.1 Encouraging Customers to Refer Others

Encouraging customers to refer others requires a proactive approach and incentives that motivate them to share your brand with their networks. Here's how you can encourage customers to refer others:

Provide Exceptional Value: Offer products or services that exceed customer expectations and provide exceptional value. Satisfied customers are more likely to recommend your brand to others.

Ask for Referrals: Actively solicit referrals from satisfied customers by asking them to share your brand with friends, family, or colleagues who may benefit from your offerings. Make it easy for customers to refer others by providing clear instructions and referral mechanisms.

Create Shareable Content: Develop shareable content such as blog posts, infographics, or videos that customers can easily share with their networks. Encourage social sharing by including social media buttons and calls-to-action in your content.

35.2 Offering Incentives for Successful Referrals

Offering incentives for successful referrals provides customers with added motivation to recommend your brand to others. Here's how you can incentivize customer referrals:

Discounts or Rewards: Offer discounts, coupons, or rewards to customers who successfully refer others to your brand. Provide incentives for both the referrer and the new subscriber to encourage participation.

Exclusive Access: Provide referrers with exclusive access to special offers, products, or events as a reward for successful referrals. Make referrers feel valued and appreciated for their advocacy.

Contests or Giveaways: Host referral contests or giveaways where customers can earn entries or prizes for each successful referral. Create excitement and competition among participants to drive engagement and participation.

35.3 Turning Referrals into Valuable Subscribers

Turning referrals into valuable subscribers requires effective follow-up and engagement strategies to convert referred leads into active subscribers. Here's how you can turn referrals into valuable subscribers:

Personalized Welcome: Provide personalized welcome messages and offers to new subscribers referred by existing customers. Acknowledge the referral and express gratitude for their interest in your brand.

Nurture Relationships: Implement email nurture campaigns to nurture relationships with referred subscribers and guide them through the customer journey. Provide valuable content, offers, and support to encourage engagement and loyalty.

Track Referral Performance: Monitor the performance of referral campaigns and track key metrics such as conversion rates, engagement, and lifetime value of referred subscribers. Use data insights to optimize your referral strategies and improve results over time.

By encouraging customers to refer others, offering incentives for successful referrals, and effectively converting referred leads into valuable subscribers, you can leverage the power of customer referrals to grow your email list and expand your customer base. Continuously refine your referral strategies based on feedback and performance data to maximize the impact of customer referrals on your email marketing efforts.

Chapter 36: Creating Email Courses and Workshops

Email courses and workshops are effective tools for providing value, educating subscribers, and growing your email list. In this chapter, we'll explore how to design educational email courses, provide value and expertise through workshops, and use these strategies to build your email list.

36.1 Designing Educational Email Courses

Designing educational email courses involves creating a series of informative and engaging emails that deliver value to subscribers over a set period. Here's how you can design effective email courses:

Define Course Objectives: Determine the objectives and goals of your email course, such as educating subscribers on a specific topic, solving a problem, or achieving a desired outcome.

Break Down Content: Break down the course content into digestible segments or lessons that can be delivered via email. Structure each lesson to provide valuable insights, actionable tips, and resources.

Set Delivery Schedule: Decide on the frequency and timing of email delivery for each lesson. Consider spacing out emails to maintain engagement and prevent overwhelm.

Include Interactive Elements: Incorporate interactive elements such as quizzes, assignments, or challenges to encourage subscriber participation and engagement.

36.2 Providing Value and Expertise through Workshops
Providing value and expertise through workshops allows you to engage with subscribers in real-time and deliver targeted, in-depth content. Here's how you can host effective workshops:

Choose Relevant Topics: Select workshop topics that are relevant to your audience's interests, pain points, or goals. Focus on areas where you can showcase your expertise and provide actionable insights.

Plan Interactive Sessions: Structure workshops to include interactive elements such as live Q&A sessions, polls, or group discussions. Encourage participation and engagement to keep attendees actively involved.

Offer Exclusive Content: Provide attendees with exclusive access to additional resources, templates, or bonus content related to the workshop topic. Make attendees feel valued and incentivized to participate.

Promote and Host: Promote workshops through your email list, social media channels, and website to attract attendees. Choose a platform or tool to host the workshop, ensuring smooth registration and participation.

36.3 Using Courses and Workshops to Build Your List

Using email courses and workshops is an effective strategy for building your email list by attracting subscribers who are interested in your content and expertise. Here's how you can leverage courses and workshops to grow your list:

Offer Free Sign-Up: Offer free sign-up for email courses and workshops to encourage registrations. Highlight the value and benefits of participating in the course or workshop to attract subscribers.

Promote Opt-In During Sessions: Promote opt-in opportunities during email courses and workshops by inviting attendees to join your email list for updates, exclusive content, or future events.

Follow Up with Additional Content: Follow up with attendees after the course or workshop by providing additional content, resources, or offers via email. Use these follow-ups to further nurture relationships and encourage subscribers to stay engaged.

By designing educational email courses, providing value and expertise through workshops, and using these strategies to build your email list, you can engage with subscribers, demonstrate your expertise, and attract new leads to your business. Continuously refine your courses and workshops based on feedback and performance data to maximize their impact on list growth and audience engagement.

Chapter 37: Leveraging User Onboarding for List Growth

User onboarding is a critical process for introducing new users to your product or service and guiding them towards success. Leveraging this process for list growth involves incorporating email capture, educating and engaging new users through emails, and converting onboarded users into subscribers.

37.1 Incorporating Email Capture in User Onboarding

Incorporating email capture into your user onboarding process allows you to seamlessly grow your email list while guiding users through the initial stages of their journey. Here's how you can effectively incorporate email capture:

Strategic Placement: Place email capture forms or opt-in prompts at strategic points in the onboarding process, such as during account registration, onboarding tutorials, or milestone achievements.

Value Proposition: Clearly communicate the value of joining your email list to users. Highlight benefits such as exclusive content, product updates, tips, or discounts to incentivize sign-ups.

Progressive Profiling: Collect additional information from users over time through progressive profiling. Start with essential information during onboarding and gradually gather more details through subsequent interactions.

37.2 Educating and Engaging New Users through Emails

Emails play a vital role in educating and engaging new users during the onboarding process. Here's how you can effectively use emails to nurture new users:

Welcome Emails: Send personalized welcome emails to new users immediately after sign-up. Introduce your brand, provide useful resources or getting started guides, and set expectations for what users can expect from your emails.

Onboarding Sequences: Create an email sequence that guides users through the onboarding process step by step. Provide educational content, tips, best practices, and tutorials to help users get the most out of your product or service.

Engagement Emails: Keep new users engaged with regular emails that provide valuable content, product updates, user success stories, or relevant resources. Encourage users to explore different features or functionalities of your product.

37.3 Converting Onboarded Users into Subscribers

Once users have completed the onboarding process, it's essential to convert them into subscribers to your email list for ongoing communication and relationship-building. Here's how you can effectively convert onboarded users into subscribers:

Exclusive Offers: Offer exclusive incentives or discounts to users who subscribe to your email list after completing the onboarding process. Highlight the value of staying connected and receiving updates, tips, and special offers.

Feedback Requests: Request feedback from onboarded users via email surveys or feedback forms. Use this opportunity to gather insights into their experience with your product or service and encourage them to join your email list for future updates and improvements.

CTAs in Product: Include clear calls-to-action (CTAs) within your product or app interface prompting users to subscribe to your email list for ongoing updates and news. Make it easy for users to opt-in directly from within the product interface.

By incorporating email capture into user onboarding, educating and engaging new users through emails, and effectively converting onboarded users into subscribers, you can leverage the onboarding process as a powerful tool for list growth. Continuously optimize your onboarding emails and strategies based on user feedback and performance data to maximize list growth and user retention over time.

Chapter 38: Gamifying the Opt-In Process

Gamifying the opt-in process involves incorporating elements of gameplay and rewards to make subscribing to your email list more interactive and engaging. In this chapter, we'll explore how to add gamification elements to opt-in forms, create interactive and rewarding experiences, and increase subscriptions through gamification.

38.1 Adding Gamification Elements to Opt-In Forms
Enhancing opt-in forms with gamification elements can capture users' attention and encourage them to subscribe to your email list. Here's how you can incorporate gamification into opt-in forms:

Progress Bars: Implement progress bars or visual indicators to show users how close they are to completing the opt-in process. Progress bars create a sense of achievement and encourage users to finish the process.

Interactive Quizzes: Integrate interactive quizzes or assessments into opt-in forms to make the subscription process more engaging. Offer rewards or incentives based on users' quiz performance or completion.

Spin-to-Win Wheels: Include spin-to-win wheels or prize wheels in opt-in forms, allowing users to spin for a chance to win discounts, freebies, or exclusive content upon subscribing to your email list.

38.2 Creating Interactive and Rewarding Experiences

Creating interactive and rewarding experiences can motivate users to interact with your opt-in forms and complete the subscription process. Here's how you can make the opt-in process more interactive and rewarding:

Unlockable Content: Offer users access to unlockable content, such as exclusive articles, guides, or videos, upon subscribing to your email list. Create anticipation and excitement by teasing the content users can unlock.

Achievement Badges: Award users with achievement badges or virtual rewards for subscribing to your email list or completing specific actions. Recognize users' progress and encourage continued engagement with your brand.

Social Sharing Challenges: Encourage users to share your opt-in forms or referral links on social media platforms to unlock special rewards or bonuses. Leverage social proof and virality to expand your reach and attract new subscribers.

38.3 Increasing Subscriptions through Gamification
Gamification can significantly increase subscriptions to your email list by making the opt-in process more enjoyable and rewarding for users. Here's how you can effectively leverage gamification to boost subscriptions:

Prominent Placement: Place gamified opt-in forms prominently on your website or landing pages to capture users' attention and encourage participation. Use eye-catching visuals and clear calls-to-action to prompt users to subscribe.

Incentivize Participation: Offer attractive incentives, rewards, or prizes to users who successfully complete the gamified opt-in process. Make the rewards relevant to users' interests and motivations to maximize participation.

Track and Analyze Performance: Monitor the performance of gamified opt-in forms using analytics tools to track conversion rates, engagement, and user behavior. Use insights to optimize your gamification strategy and improve subscription rates over time.

By adding gamification elements to opt-in forms, creating interactive and rewarding experiences, and effectively incentivizing participation, you can increase subscriptions to your email list and enhance user engagement with your brand. Continuously iterate and refine your gamification strategy based on user feedback and performance data to maximize its effectiveness in driving conversions and growing your email list.

Chapter 39: Engaging Subscribers with Exclusive Content

Engaging subscribers with exclusive content is a powerful strategy for nurturing relationships, increasing loyalty, and driving conversions. In this chapter, we'll explore how to offer premium content to email subscribers, create a sense of exclusivity and VIP access, and retain subscribers through exclusive benefits.

39.1 Offering Premium Content to Email Subscribers
Offering premium content exclusively to email subscribers provides added value and incentive for users to join your email list. Here's how you can offer premium content to subscribers:

Ebooks and Guides: Create comprehensive ebooks, guides, or whitepapers on topics relevant to your audience's interests or pain points. Offer these resources exclusively to email subscribers as a reward for signing up.

Webinars and Workshops: Host exclusive webinars or workshops for email subscribers, featuring expert insights, industry trends, or actionable strategies. Provide subscribers with early access or priority registration to these events.

Exclusive Discounts: Offer exclusive discounts, promotions, or special offers to email subscribers as a perk for being part of your community. Make subscribers feel valued and appreciated by providing access to deals they can't find elsewhere.

39.2 Creating a Sense of Exclusivity and VIP Access

Creating a sense of exclusivity and VIP access for email subscribers enhances their experience and fosters a stronger connection with your brand. Here's how you can create a sense of exclusivity:

VIP Clubs or Memberships: Create VIP clubs or membership programs for email subscribers, offering special privileges, perks, or rewards for joining. Provide exclusive access to premium content, events, or product releases reserved for VIP members.

Early Access: Offer email subscribers early access to new products, features, or content before it's available to the public. Make subscribers feel like insiders by providing them with exclusive previews or sneak peeks.

Limited-Time Offers: Introduce limited-time offers or flash sales exclusively for email subscribers, creating a sense of urgency and exclusivity. Encourage subscribers to take advantage of these exclusive opportunities before they expire.

39.3 Retaining Subscribers through Exclusive Benefits

Retaining subscribers over the long term requires continuously providing value and exclusive benefits to keep them engaged and invested in your brand. Here's how you can retain subscribers through exclusive benefits:

Regular Updates: Send regular updates and exclusive content to email subscribers to keep them informed and engaged. Provide valuable insights, tips, or behind-the-scenes content that's not available elsewhere.

Surprise Rewards: Surprise subscribers with unexpected rewards or gifts as a token of appreciation for their continued loyalty. Offer exclusive discounts, freebies, or access to special events to show your gratitude.

Feedback Opportunities: Solicit feedback from email subscribers and involve them in shaping the direction of your brand or content. Offer exclusive opportunities for subscribers to participate in surveys, polls, or focus groups to make them feel valued and heard.

By offering premium content to email subscribers, creating a sense of exclusivity and VIP access, and retaining subscribers through exclusive benefits, you can strengthen relationships, increase loyalty, and drive long-term engagement with your audience. Continuously evaluate and refine your exclusive content strategy based on subscriber feedback and performance metrics to maximize its effectiveness in nurturing relationships and driving results.

Chapter 40: Leveraging Podcasts for List Building

Podcasts have become a popular medium for reaching and engaging audiences, making them an effective tool for list building. In this chapter, we'll explore how to leverage podcasts to grow your email list, promote opt-in opportunities within podcast episodes, and convert podcast listeners into subscribers.

40.1 Starting a Podcast to Grow Your Email List

Starting a podcast offers a unique opportunity to connect with your target audience and promote your brand while simultaneously growing your email list. Here's how you can use podcasts to grow your email list:

Identify Your Niche: Choose a podcast topic that aligns with your brand and appeals to your target audience's interests. Focus on providing valuable content that educates, entertains, or inspires listeners.

Promote Opt-In Incentives: Promote opt-in incentives or lead magnets within your podcast episodes to encourage listeners to subscribe to your email list. Offer exclusive content, resources, or discounts related to the podcast topic to entice sign-ups.

Include Call-to-Actions (CTAs): Include clear and compelling CTAs within your podcast episodes, prompting listeners to visit your website or landing page to subscribe to your email list. Reinforce the value of subscribing and provide easy-to-follow instructions for signing up.

40.2 Promoting Opt-In Opportunities within Podcast Episodes

Promoting opt-in opportunities within podcast episodes is an effective way to capture the interest of listeners and convert them into email subscribers. Here are some strategies for promoting opt-in opportunities within your podcast episodes:

Mention Lead Magnets: Mention lead magnets or opt-in incentives at the beginning, middle, or end of your podcast episodes. Highlight the benefits of subscribing to your email list and provide a compelling reason for listeners to take action.

Use Dynamic Ad Inserts: Insert dynamic ad spots or sponsorships within your podcast episodes to promote opt-in opportunities. Customize ad content to align with the podcast topic and audience interests, making it relevant and engaging for listeners.

Guest Collaborations: Collaborate with guests or experts within your podcast episodes to promote opt-in opportunities. Encourage guests to share their expertise and offer exclusive resources or content to listeners who subscribe to your email list.

40.3 Converting Podcast Listeners into Subscribers

Converting podcast listeners into email subscribers requires strategic follow-up and engagement tactics to drive conversions. Here's how you can convert podcast listeners into subscribers:

Follow-Up Emails: Follow up with listeners after they've listened to your podcast episodes by sending targeted follow-up emails. Thank them for listening, provide additional value or resources, and invite them to subscribe to your email list for more content.

Create Podcast-Specific Content: Create podcast-specific content or bonus episodes that are exclusive to email subscribers. Encourage listeners to subscribe to your email list to access this exclusive content and stay updated on future episodes.

Engage on Social Media: Engage with listeners on social media platforms to continue the conversation beyond the podcast episode. Encourage followers to join your email list for exclusive updates, behind-the-scenes content, or special offers.

By starting a podcast to grow your email list, promoting opt-in opportunities within podcast episodes, and strategically converting podcast listeners into subscribers, you can effectively leverage podcasts as a powerful tool for list building and audience engagement. Continuously refine your podcasting strategy based on listener feedback and performance metrics to maximize its impact on list growth and audience retention.

Chapter 41: Implementing SMS Marketing for List Growth

Implementing SMS marketing can be a highly effective strategy for list growth, allowing you to reach audiences directly on their mobile devices. In this chapter, we'll explore how to utilize SMS opt-in and subscription strategies, send targeted and engaging SMS campaigns, and integrate SMS and email marketing efforts for maximum impact.

41.1 Utilizing SMS Opt-In and Subscription Strategies

Utilizing effective SMS opt-in and subscription strategies is crucial for building a quality SMS marketing list. Here's how you can encourage users to opt-in to your SMS list:

Clear Opt-In Forms: Provide clear and concise opt-in forms on your website, social media channels, or other marketing materials. Clearly communicate the benefits of subscribing to your SMS list and obtain explicit consent from users.

Incentives and Offers: Offer incentives or exclusive offers to users who opt-in to your SMS list, such as discounts, freebies, or early access to promotions. Make the value proposition compelling to encourage sign-ups.

Keyword Campaigns: Run keyword campaigns where users can text a specific keyword to a designated number to opt-in to your SMS list. Promote these campaigns across various channels and incentivize participation with exclusive content or rewards.

41.2 Sending Targeted and Engaging SMS Campaigns

Sending targeted and engaging SMS campaigns is essential for maintaining subscriber interest and driving conversions. Here are some strategies for creating effective SMS campaigns:

Segmentation: Segment your SMS list based on user demographics, preferences, or past interactions to send targeted messages that resonate with specific segments of your audience.

Personalization: Personalize your SMS messages with the recipient's name or other relevant information to create a more personalized and engaging experience. Use dynamic content to tailor messages based on user behavior or preferences.

Compelling Content: Keep SMS messages concise, informative, and engaging. Use compelling language, emojis, or multimedia content to capture attention and encourage interaction with your messages.

41.3 Integrating SMS and Email Marketing Efforts

Integrating SMS and email marketing efforts allows you to create cohesive multi-channel campaigns and maximize the impact of your marketing efforts. Here's how you can integrate SMS and email marketing efforts:

Cross-Promotion: Cross-promote your SMS and email marketing efforts to encourage subscribers to engage with both channels. Include calls-to-action in your email campaigns prompting subscribers to opt-in to your SMS list, and vice versa.

Coordinated Campaigns: Coordinate SMS and email campaigns to deliver consistent messaging and reinforce brand identity across channels. Use SMS to send timely reminders or follow-ups to email campaigns, increasing touchpoints with subscribers.

Data Synchronization: Ensure that subscriber data is synchronized between your SMS and email marketing platforms to provide a seamless experience for users. Keep track of subscriber preferences, interactions, and campaign performance across both channels.

By utilizing SMS opt-in and subscription strategies, sending targeted and engaging SMS campaigns, and integrating SMS and email marketing efforts, you can effectively leverage SMS marketing for list growth and audience engagement. Continuously analyze performance metrics and refine your SMS marketing strategy to optimize results and maximize ROI.

Chapter 42: Utilizing Lead Ads on Social Media

Utilizing lead ads on social media platforms like Facebook can be a powerful way to grow your email list. In this chapter, we'll explore how to leverage Facebook lead ads for list building, design effective lead ad campaigns, and automate lead ad responses and follow-ups.

42.1 Leveraging Facebook Lead Ads for List Building

Facebook lead ads provide a streamlined way to collect information from users and grow your email list directly on the platform. Here's how you can leverage Facebook lead ads for list building:

Simple Opt-In Process: Facebook lead ads simplify the opt-in process by allowing users to sign up for your email list without leaving the Facebook platform. This reduces friction and makes it easier for users to subscribe.

Customizable Forms: Customize lead ad forms to collect the information you need from subscribers, such as their name, email address, and any additional details relevant to your business or campaign.

Integration with CRM Systems: Integrate Facebook lead ads with your CRM system or email marketing platform to automatically sync new leads and streamline your list building process.

42.2 Designing Effective Lead Ad Campaigns

Designing effective lead ad campaigns is crucial for capturing users' attention and encouraging them to subscribe to your email list. Here's how you can design compelling lead ad campaigns:

Compelling Ad Copy: Write attention-grabbing ad copy that clearly communicates the benefits of subscribing to your email list. Highlight what subscribers will receive and why they should sign up.

Eye-Catching Visuals: Use high-quality images or videos that resonate with your target audience and complement your ad copy. Visuals can help make your lead ads more engaging and memorable.

Clear Call-to-Action (CTA): Include a clear and compelling call-to-action (CTA) in your lead ads, prompting users to take action and sign up for your email list. Use actionable language and make it easy for users to understand what they need to do.

42.3 Automating Lead Ad Responses and Follow-ups

Automating lead ad responses and follow-ups can help streamline your lead generation process and ensure timely communication with new subscribers. Here's how you can automate lead ad responses and follow-ups:

Instant Replies: Set up instant replies to thank users for signing up and provide any additional information or resources they may need. Instant replies help create a positive first impression and keep users engaged.

Follow-Up Emails: Create automated follow-up email sequences to nurture new leads and further engage them with your brand. Tailor your follow-up emails based on users' interests or actions to provide personalized experiences.

Lead Segmentation: Use lead segmentation to categorize new leads based on their interests, demographics, or behaviors. This allows you to send targeted follow-up messages that are relevant to each segment, increasing the likelihood of conversion.

By leveraging Facebook lead ads for list building, designing effective lead ad campaigns, and automating lead ad responses and follow-ups, you can effectively grow your email list and nurture relationships with new subscribers. Continuously monitor and optimize your lead ad campaigns to improve performance and maximize results over time.

Chapter 43: Engaging Subscribers through Interactive Email Campaigns

Interactive email campaigns are an innovative way to captivate your audience and foster deeper engagement with your brand. In this chapter, we'll explore how to incorporate interactive elements into your email campaigns, encourage subscriber participation and feedback, and ultimately increase engagement and list growth through interactivity.

43.1 Incorporating Interactive Elements in Email Campaigns

Incorporating interactive elements into your email campaigns can significantly enhance the user experience and encourage recipients to interact with your content. Here's how you can leverage interactivity:

Interactive Images and GIFs: Use dynamic images and GIFs to capture attention and convey messages in a more engaging manner. Animated elements can help draw focus to key points and encourage recipients to take action.

Polls and Surveys: Embed polls or surveys directly into your emails to gather feedback and insights from subscribers. Encourage recipients to share their opinions and preferences, fostering a sense of involvement and community.

Clickable CTAs: Make your calls-to-action (CTAs) more interactive by using buttons or clickable elements that prompt immediate action. Experiment with different designs and wording to optimize click-through rates and conversions.

43.2 Encouraging Subscriber Participation and Feedback

Encouraging subscriber participation and feedback is essential for building a strong rapport with your audience and fostering a sense of ownership. Here's how you can facilitate engagement:

Interactive Quizzes and Games: Create interactive quizzes or games that challenge recipients and provide entertainment value. Offer incentives or rewards for participation to incentivize engagement and drive interaction.

Feedback Loops: Establish feedback loops where subscribers can share their thoughts, suggestions, and experiences directly with your brand. Actively listen to feedback and use it to inform future email campaigns and product improvements.

User-Generated Content: Encourage subscribers to contribute user-generated content, such as testimonials, reviews, or user-generated photos, that can be featured in your email campaigns. This not only adds authenticity but also fosters a sense of community.

43.3 Increasing Engagement and List Growth with Interactivity

Increasing engagement and list growth through interactivity requires a strategic approach that prioritizes user experience and value delivery. Here's how you can achieve this:

Exclusive Interactive Content: Offer exclusive interactive content to email subscribers, such as interactive eBooks, virtual tours, or interactive infographics, that can't be accessed elsewhere. Highlight the unique value proposition of subscribing to your email list.

Social Sharing and Virality: Incorporate interactive elements that encourage social sharing and virality, such as interactive challenges or quizzes that recipients can easily share with their social networks. Leverage the power of social proof to attract new subscribers organically.

Segmentation and Personalization: Segment your email list based on subscriber preferences and behaviors to deliver personalized interactive experiences. Tailor content and interactive elements to each segment's interests and needs, increasing relevance and engagement.

By incorporating interactive elements into your email campaigns, encouraging subscriber participation and feedback, and focusing on increasing engagement and list growth through interactivity, you can create more compelling and memorable experiences for your audience. Continuously test and optimize your interactive email strategies to drive better results and foster deeper connections with your subscribers.

Chapter 44: Building Partnerships with Non-Competitive Businesses

Collaborating with non-competitive businesses can offer a multitude of benefits, including expanded reach, shared resources, and increased brand credibility. In this chapter, we'll explore how to identify opportunities for partnerships, collaborate on joint marketing initiatives, and leverage strategic partnerships to grow your business.

44.1 Identifying Non-Competitive Business Opportunities
Identifying opportunities for partnerships with non-competitive businesses involves finding synergies and complementary aspects between your offerings. Here's how you can identify these opportunities:

Market Research: Conduct thorough market research to identify businesses that share a similar target audience but offer complementary products or services. Look for businesses that cater to the same demographic or solve adjacent problems.

Networking Events: Attend industry events, conferences, or networking meetups to connect with potential partners in your niche or related industries. Strike up conversations and explore potential collaboration opportunities based on mutual interests and goals.

Online Communities: Join online forums, social media groups, or industry-specific communities where businesses gather to discuss challenges and share insights. Engage with members and look for opportunities to collaborate on joint   initiatives   or   projects.

44.2 Collaborating on Joint Marketing Initiatives

Collaborating on joint marketing initiatives allows you to pool resources, amplify your reach, and achieve mutual marketing objectives. Here's how you can collaborate effectively:

Co-branded Campaigns: Create co-branded marketing campaigns or promotions that leverage the strengths of both businesses. Develop compelling offers or content that resonates with your shared audience and promotes both brands simultaneously.

Cross-promotion: Cross-promote each other's products or services through email newsletters, social media channels, or blog posts. Highlight the value proposition of partnering with the other business and offer exclusive discounts or incentives to drive conversions.

Event Sponsorship: Sponsor or co-host events, webinars, or workshops with your partner to showcase your expertise and engage with a broader audience. Collaborate on event planning, promotion, and content creation to maximize impact.

44.3 Expanding Your Reach through Strategic Partnerships

Strategic partnerships enable you to tap into new markets, access new customer segments, and expand your reach beyond your existing network. Here's how you can leverage strategic partnerships:

Referral Programs: Establish referral programs with your partners where you incentivize each other's customers to refer new business. Offer rewards or discounts for successful referrals, creating a win-win situation for both businesses.

Content Collaboration: Collaborate on content creation initiatives, such as guest blog posts, co-authored eBooks, or joint webinars. By sharing your expertise and resources, you can create valuable content that resonates with a wider audience and drives engagement.

Product Integration: Explore opportunities for product integration or bundling where your offerings complement each other. Integrate your products or services to provide a more comprehensive solution to customers, adding value and differentiation.

By identifying non-competitive business opportunities, collaborating on joint marketing initiatives, and leveraging strategic partnerships, you can unlock new growth opportunities and strengthen your position in the market. Continuously nurture and maintain your partnerships to ensure long-term success and mutual benefit.

Chapter 45: Using Chatbots for List Building

Chatbots have revolutionized customer engagement by providing personalized interactions and automating processes. In this chapter, we'll explore how to harness the power of chatbots for lead generation, engaging users, collecting email addresses, and integrating chatbot data with email marketing efforts.

45.1 Implementing Chatbots for Lead Generation

Implementing chatbots for lead generation involves setting up automated conversational experiences that prompt users to provide their contact information. Here's how you can do it:

Chatbot Setup: Choose a chatbot platform or tool that aligns with your business needs and objectives. Configure your chatbot to initiate conversations with website visitors or social media users and guide them through the lead generation process.

Lead Qualification: Design chatbot conversations to qualify leads based on predefined criteria, such as demographics, interests, or purchase intent. Use branching logic and conditional responses to tailor conversations to each user's unique profile and preferences.

Data Capture: Prompt users to provide their contact information, such as name and email address, during the chatbot conversation. Make the process seamless and user-friendly to maximize conversions and minimize friction.

45.2 Engaging Users and Collecting Email Addresses

Engaging users and collecting email addresses through chatbots requires a strategic approach that focuses on providing value and building rapport. Here's how you can achieve this:

Interactive Content: Create interactive chatbot experiences that offer value to users, such as quizzes, assessments, or personalized recommendations. Use these interactions to gather insights about users' preferences and interests, which can inform your email marketing efforts.

Lead Magnets: Offer lead magnets or incentives, such as exclusive content, discounts, or freebies, to users who provide their email addresses through the chatbot. Highlight the benefits of subscribing to your email list and make it irresistible for users to opt-in.

Natural Language Processing (NLP): Implement natural language processing capabilities in your chatbot to enable more natural and conversational interactions. Use AI-powered responses to understand users' intents and provide relevant information or assistance.

45.3 Integrating Chatbot Data with Email Marketing Efforts

Integrating chatbot data with email marketing efforts allows you to leverage the insights gathered from chatbot interactions to personalize and optimize your email campaigns. Here's how you can do it:

Data Segmentation: Segment your email list based on the data collected from chatbot interactions, such as user preferences, behavior patterns, or engagement level. Use segmentation to deliver targeted and relevant email content that resonates with each segment.

Personalization: Personalize your email campaigns based on the information gathered by the chatbot, such as addressing users by name or recommending products or content based on their interests. Tailor your messaging to create a more personalized and engaging experience for subscribers.

Automation: Set up automated email workflows triggered by specific chatbot interactions or user actions. Use automated emails to nurture leads, deliver content, or follow up on inquiries, increasing engagement and driving conversions over time.

By implementing chatbots for lead generation, engaging users, collecting email addresses, and integrating chatbot data with email marketing efforts, you can create seamless and personalized experiences that drive list growth and foster meaningful connections with your audience. Continuously monitor and optimize your chatbot and email marketing strategies to maximize results and achieve your business objectives.

Chapter 46: Maximizing Email List Building with Influencer Takeovers

Influencer takeovers offer a unique opportunity to leverage the reach and credibility of influencers to grow your email list. In this chapter, we'll explore how to effectively utilize influencer takeovers for list growth, plan and execute successful takeover campaigns, and convert influencer audiences into subscribers.

46.1 Leveraging Influencer Takeovers for List Growth

Influencer takeovers involve inviting influencers to temporarily control your email or social media channels to engage with your audience. Here's how you can leverage influencer takeovers for list growth:

Audience Reach: Identify influencers whose audience demographics align with your target market. Collaborate with influencers who have a sizable and engaged following to maximize the reach of your takeover campaign.

Credibility and Trust: Leverage the credibility and trust that influencers have built with their audience. When influencers endorse your brand or promote your email list, their followers are more likely to trust their recommendation and subscribe to your list.

Content Variety: Introduce variety into your email content by featuring influencers' unique perspectives, expertise, or behind-the-scenes insights. This can help attract new subscribers who are interested in the influencer's content and want to stay updated on future collaborations.

46.2 Planning and Executing Successful Takeover Campaigns

Planning and executing successful influencer takeover campaigns require careful coordination and alignment with your marketing goals. Here's how you can plan and execute a successful takeover campaign:

Goal Setting: Clearly define your objectives for the takeover campaign, whether it's to increase email subscribers, drive traffic to your website, or promote a specific product or service. Establish key performance indicators (KPIs) to measure the success of the campaign.

Content Strategy: Collaborate with the influencer to develop a content strategy that resonates with their audience while aligning with your brand messaging and goals. Determine the type of content to be shared during the takeover, such as exclusive offers, behind-the-scenes content, or Q&A sessions.

Promotion and Timing: Promote the takeover campaign across your email list, social media channels, and other marketing channels to generate anticipation and excitement. Coordinate with the influencer to schedule the takeover at a time when their audience is most active and engaged.

46.3 Converting Influencer Audience into Subscribers

Converting the influencer's audience into subscribers requires a strategic approach to engage and incentivize them to join your email list. Here's how you can convert the influencer's audience into subscribers:

Opt-In Incentives: Offer exclusive opt-in incentives or rewards to the influencer's audience, such as discounts, freebies, or access to gated content. Make subscribing to your email list a valuable and enticing proposition for the influencer's followers.

Call-to-Action (CTA): Include clear and compelling calls-to-action (CTAs) throughout the takeover content, prompting the influencer's audience to subscribe to your email list. Use persuasive language and visuals to encourage immediate action.

Follow-Up Engagement: Nurture new subscribers with engaging email content and personalized follow-up messages. Provide value, build trust, and cultivate relationships with the influencer's audience to encourage long-term engagement and loyalty.

By leveraging influencer takeovers for list growth, planning and executing successful takeover campaigns, and converting the influencer's audience into subscribers, you can maximize the impact of your email list building efforts and expand your reach to new audiences. Continuously evaluate and optimize your influencer marketing strategies to drive sustainable growth and achieve your marketing objectives.

Chapter 47: Harnessing the Power of Online Communities

Online communities provide fertile ground for cultivating relationships, fostering engagement, and driving email list growth. In this chapter, we'll delve into how to build and engage online communities, promote opt-in opportunities within these communities, and nurture community members into subscribers.

47.1 Building and Engaging Online Communities

Building and engaging online communities involves creating spaces where like-minded individuals can connect, share insights, and support each other. Here's how you can do it effectively:

Choose the Right Platform: Select a platform that aligns with your audience's preferences and interests. Whether it's a forum, social media group, or specialized community platform, choose a platform where your target audience is most active.

Create Valuable Content: Share valuable content within the community that educates, entertains, or inspires members. Offer insights, tips, or resources that address their pain points or interests, positioning yourself as a trusted authority within the community.

Encourage Interaction: Foster interaction and engagement within the community by asking questions, initiating discussions, and soliciting feedback from members. Encourage members to share their experiences, ask questions, and support each other.

47.2 Promoting Opt-In Opportunities within Communities

Promoting opt-in opportunities within online communities allows you to capture leads directly from engaged members. Here's how you can promote opt-in opportunities effectively:

Offer Exclusive Content: Provide exclusive content or resources to community members who opt-in to your email list. Highlight the value of subscribing and emphasize the benefits of accessing exclusive content.

Host Webinars or Workshops: Organize webinars, workshops, or training sessions within the community and require participants to opt-in to your email list to attend. Use these events to deliver value and showcase your expertise while growing your list.

Run Contests or Giveaways: Run contests or giveaways within the community and require participants to subscribe to your email list for a chance to win. Use enticing prizes and compelling calls-to-action to encourage opt-ins.

47.3 Nurturing Community Members into Subscribers

Nurturing community members into subscribers involves building relationships, providing value, and guiding them through the opt-in process. Here's how you can nurture community members into subscribers:

Provide Value First: Focus on providing value and building trust with community members before promoting opt-in opportunities. Establish yourself as a helpful resource and engage with members authentically.

Share Testimonials or Case Studies: Share testimonials or case studies from satisfied subscribers within the community to demonstrate the value of subscribing to your email list. Highlight success stories and benefits to incentivize opt-ins.

Offer Incentives: Offer incentives or rewards to community members who subscribe to your email list, such as discounts, freebies, or exclusive access to content. Make subscribing irresistible by offering tangible benefits.

By harnessing the power of online communities, promoting opt-in opportunities within these communities, and nurturing community members into subscribers, you can leverage engaged audiences to grow your email list and foster meaningful connections with your audience. Continuously engage with community members, provide value, and optimize your strategies to drive list growth and achieve your marketing objectives.

Chapter 48: Leveraging User-generated Social Proof

User-generated social proof is a powerful tool for building trust, credibility, and ultimately, growing your email list. In this chapter, we'll explore how to collect and showcase user-generated social proof, use it to increase trust and conversions, and incorporate it into your email list building efforts.

48.1 Collecting and Showcasing User-generated Social Proof

Collecting and showcasing user-generated social proof involves leveraging the positive experiences and testimonials of your existing customers or users. Here's how you can do it effectively:

Customer Testimonials: Encourage satisfied customers to share their experiences and testimonials about your products or services. Collect these testimonials through surveys, reviews, or feedback forms, and showcase them prominently on your website, social media channels, and marketing materials.

User-generated Content: Encourage users to create and share content related to your brand or products, such as photos, videos, or reviews. Feature user-generated content on your website, social media profiles, and email newsletters to demonstrate real-life use cases and experiences.

Social Media Mentions: Monitor social media platforms for mentions, tags, or posts related to your brand or products. Repurpose positive social media mentions and user-generated content in your marketing efforts to amplify positive sentiment and build credibility.

48.2 Using Social Proof to Increase Trust and Conversions

Social proof serves as a powerful psychological cue that influences people's perceptions and decisions. Here's how you can leverage social proof to increase trust and conversions:

Peer Influence: Highlight the popularity and positive experiences of other customers or users to influence prospects' decisions. Use social proof elements such as ratings, reviews, and testimonials to reassure prospects and alleviate any doubts or concerns they may have.

Authority Endorsements: Showcase endorsements or testimonials from industry influencers, experts, or recognizable brands to lend credibility and authority to your offerings. People are more likely to trust recommendations from authoritative figures or brands they admire.

FOMO (Fear of Missing Out): Create a sense of urgency and scarcity by showcasing social proof elements such as limited stock availability, high demand, or time-limited offers. Use phrases like "Join thousands of satisfied customers" or "Limited spots available" to trigger FOMO and drive conversions.

48.3 Incorporating Social Proof in Email List Building Efforts

Incorporating social proof into your email list building efforts can enhance the effectiveness of your opt-in incentives and calls-to-action. Here's how you can do it:

Testimonial Sign-up Forms: Include customer testimonials or reviews near your email sign-up forms to reassure visitors and increase trust. Highlight the benefits of subscribing and showcase social proof to incentivize opt-ins.

Social Proof Emails: Send emails featuring user-generated content, testimonials, or social proof elements to subscribers to reinforce their decision to join your email list. Use social proof to validate subscribers' choice and reaffirm the value of being part of your community.

Referral Programs: Encourage existing subscribers to refer friends or colleagues to join your email list by offering incentives or rewards. Showcase social proof elements such as the number of subscribers or testimonials from satisfied subscribers to incentivize referrals.

By leveraging user-generated social proof, you can build trust, credibility, and authority in your brand, ultimately driving conversions and growing your email list.

Incorporate social proof strategically into your marketing efforts to maximize its impact and foster stronger connections with your audience.

Chapter 49: Optimizing Mobile Experience for List Building

In today's mobile-first world, optimizing the mobile experience for list building is essential for capturing leads and engaging with your audience effectively. In this chapter, we'll explore how to design mobile-friendly opt-in forms and pages, streamline the mobile email subscription process, and maximize list growth through mobile optimization.

49.1 Designing Mobile-Friendly Opt-In Forms and Pages

Designing mobile-friendly opt-in forms and pages is crucial for ensuring a seamless user experience on mobile devices. Here's how you can do it effectively:

Responsive Design: Use responsive design techniques to ensure that opt-in forms and landing pages adapt and display correctly on various screen sizes and devices. Test your forms and pages across different mobile devices to ensure consistency and usability.

Clear and Concise Copy: Keep your opt-in form copy clear, concise, and easy to read on mobile devices. Use short and compelling headlines, bullet points, and minimalistic design elements to convey your message effectively without overwhelming mobile users.

Large and Tappable Buttons: Make sure that opt-in buttons are large enough and easily tappable on touch screens. Use contrasting colors and ample white space to make buttons stand out and encourage clicks from mobile users.

49.2 Streamlining Mobile Email Subscription Process

Streamlining the mobile email subscription process is essential for reducing friction and increasing conversions on mobile devices. Here's how you can streamline the process:

Single-step Opt-ins: Minimize the number of steps required for users to subscribe to your email list on mobile devices. Implement single-step opt-in forms that capture essential information (e.g., email address) directly within the form without redirecting users to additional pages.

Social Media Sign-up Options: Offer social media sign-up options that allow users to subscribe to your email list with just a few taps using their existing social media accounts. Streamline the sign-up process by pre-filling form fields with data from users' social media profiles.

Auto-fill and Autofocus: Enable auto-fill and autofocus features on your opt-in forms to make it easier for users to complete the subscription process on mobile devices. Pre-fill form fields with default values or user data whenever possible to save time and effort.

49.3 Maximizing List Growth through Mobile Optimization

Maximizing list growth through mobile optimization requires a holistic approach that focuses on providing value and convenience to mobile users. Here's how you can do it:

Optimize Email Content for Mobile: Ensure that your email content is optimized for mobile devices, including responsive design, concise copy, and mobile-friendly images. Use mobile-responsive email templates and test your emails across various mobile devices and email clients.

Mobile-specific Offers: Create special offers or incentives specifically targeted at mobile users to encourage them to subscribe to your email list. Offer exclusive discounts, freebies, or content upgrades that are accessible and redeemable on mobile devices.

Track and Analyze Mobile Performance: Use analytics tools to track and analyze the performance of your mobile opt-in forms, landing pages, and email campaigns. Monitor key metrics such as conversion rates, click-through rates, and bounce rates to identify areas for improvement and optimization.

By designing mobile-friendly opt-in forms and pages, streamlining the mobile email subscription process, and maximizing list growth through mobile optimization, you can create a seamless and engaging experience for mobile users and drive significant growth in your email list.

Prioritize mobile optimization in your list building efforts to reach and connect with a broader audience effectively.

Chapter 50: Continuous Testing, Tracking, and Optimization

Continuous testing, tracking, and optimization are essential components of a successful email list building strategy. In this chapter, we'll explore the importance of testing and optimization, tracking key metrics, analyzing results, and implementing iterative improvements for long-term success.

50.1 Importance of Testing and Optimization for List Building

Testing and optimization play a crucial role in maximizing the effectiveness of your list building efforts. Here's why testing and optimization are essential:

Optimizing Conversion Rates: By testing different elements of your opt-in forms, landing pages, and email campaigns, you can identify what resonates best with your audience and optimize for higher conversion rates.

Improving User Experience: Continuous testing allows you to refine the user experience across various touchpoints, ensuring that the opt-in process is seamless, intuitive, and user-friendly.

Staying Competitive: In a constantly evolving digital landscape, testing and optimization are essential for staying ahead of the competition. By continuously refining your strategies, you can adapt to changing trends and consumer preferences more effectively.

50.2 Tracking Key Metrics and Analyzing Results

Tracking key metrics and analyzing results provide valuable insights into the performance of your list building efforts. Here are some key metrics to track and analyze:

Conversion Rate: Monitor the conversion rate of your opt-in forms and landing pages to assess their effectiveness in capturing leads.

Click-Through Rate (CTR): Track the CTR of your email campaigns to gauge engagement and identify areas for improvement in your email marketing strategy.

Subscriber Growth: Keep track of the growth rate of your email list over time to measure the success of your list building efforts.

Engagement Metrics: Monitor engagement metrics such as open rates, click rates, and unsubscribe rates to evaluate the effectiveness of your email campaigns and content.

Segment Performance: Analyze the performance of different audience segments to identify patterns, preferences, and opportunities for personalization.

50.3 Implementing Iterative Improvements for Long-Term Success

Continuous testing and optimization involve implementing iterative improvements based on data-driven insights. Here's how you can implement iterative improvements for long-term success:

A/B Testing: Conduct A/B tests on different elements of your opt-in forms, landing pages, and email campaigns to compare performance and identify winning variations.

Iterative Design: Continuously iterate on the design and functionality of your opt-in forms, landing pages, and emails based on user feedback, best practices, and evolving trends.

Data-driven Decisions: Make informed decisions based on data and analytics rather than assumptions or intuition. Use insights from testing and tracking to guide your optimization efforts and prioritize areas for improvement.

Continuous Learning: Stay informed about industry trends, best practices, and emerging technologies in email marketing and list building. Invest in ongoing education and training to enhance your skills and stay ahead of the curve.

By embracing a culture of continuous testing, tracking, and optimization, you can refine your email list building strategy over time, drive significant improvements in performance, and achieve long-term success in growing and nurturing your email list. Regularly review your results, iterate on your strategies, and stay adaptable to changes in the digital landscape to maintain a competitive edge and maximize the impact of your email marketing efforts.

As we reach the culmination of this journey into the realm of email list building mastery, I implore you to remember one timeless truth: the power to transform your dreams into reality lies within your grasp.

In the vast expanse of cyberspace, where possibilities are as infinite as the stars, your email list serves as the conduit through which you can connect, inspire, and elevate those who embark on this journey alongside you.

But remember, dear reader, that the journey doesn't end here. It is merely a stepping stone, a catalyst for your relentless pursuit of excellence. As you navigate the ever-shifting currents of digital marketing, may you harness the knowledge gleaned from these pages to chart your course with unwavering determination and boundless creativity.

In the realm of email list building, each subscriber is not merely a number, but a beacon of potential waiting to be ignited. With every click, every open, and every conversion, you have the power to ignite change, inspire action, and leave an indelible mark upon the digital landscape.

So, as you venture forth into the vast unknown, armed with the wisdom and insights bestowed upon you, remember this: the greatest achievements are born not from complacency, but from the relentless pursuit of excellence.

Go forth, dear reader, and may your email list be a testament to your ambition, your ingenuity, and your unyielding resolve to unlock the boundless potential that lies within. For in the realm of email list building, the journey is as exhilarating as the destination, and the possibilities are truly endless.

RK. Iskandar

www.ingramcontent.com/pod-product-compliance
Lightning Source LLC
Chambersburg PA
CBHW060451290526
45791CB00001B/68